AS WE THINK,
SO WE ARE

OTHER TITLES IN THE

LIBRARY OF
HIDDEN KNOWLEDGE

The New Master Key System

The New Science of Getting Rich

Natural Abundance

The New Game of Life and How to Play It

Coming in 2013

One Law:
Henry Drummond on Nature's Law, Spirit, and Love

As We Think, So We Are

JAMES ALLEN'S GUIDE TO TRANSFORMING OUR LIVES

edited by RUTH L. MILLER

LIBRARY OF
HIDDEN KNOWLEDGE

ATRIA BOOKS
New York London Toronto Sydney New Delhi

BEYOND WORDS
Hillsboro, Oregon

ATRIA BOOKS
A Division of Simon & Schuster, Inc.
1230 Avenue of the Americas
New York, NY 10020

BEYOND WORDS
20827 N.W. Cornell Road, Suite 500
Hillsboro, Oregon 97124-9808
503-531-8700 / 503-531-8773 fax
www.beyondword.com

Copyright © 2012 by Atria Books/Beyond Words Publishing, Inc.

Original text for *As We Think, So We Are* from the James Allen Free Library.
http://james-allen.in1woord.nl/

Managing editor: Lindsay S. Brown
Editor: Henry Covey
Copyeditor: Jade Chan
Proofreader: Susan Lynch, Jennifer Weaver-Neist
Design: Devon Smith
Composition: William H. Brunson Typography Services

First Atria Books/Beyond Words hardcover edition October 2012

ATRIA BOOKS and colophon are trademarks of Simon & Schuster, Inc. Beyond Words Publishing is an imprint of Simon & Schuster, Inc., and the Beyond Words logo is a registered trademark of Beyond Words Publishing, Inc.

For more information about special discounts for bulk purchases, please contact Simon & Schuster Special Sales at 1-866-506-1949 or business@simonandschuster.com.

The Simon & Schuster Speakers Bureau can bring authors to your live event. For more information or to book an event, contact the Simon & Schuster Speakers Bureau at 1-866-248-3049 or visit our website at www.simonspeakers.com.

Manufactured in the United States of America

10 9 8 7 6 5 4 3 2

Library of Congress Cataloging-in-Publication Data
Allen, James, 1864–1912.
    As we think, so we are : James Allen's guide to transforming our lives / edited by Ruth L. Miller.
        p.   cm. — (Library of hidden knowledge)
    Includes bibliographical references.
        1. New Thought.   2. Conduct of life.   I. Miller, Ruth L., 1948–   II. Allen, James, 1864-1912 As a man thinketh.   III. Title.
    BF639.A485   2012
    289.9′8—dc23

2012016160

ISBN: 978-1-58270-375-6
ISBN: 978-1-4516-8191-8 (ebook)

The corporate mission of Beyond Words Publishing, Inc.: *Inspire to Integrity*

The dreamers are the saviors of the word.

—James Allen

From *As A Man Thinketh* (1903)

CONTENTS

To Rise Above

ORIGINAL TEXT

As a Man Thinketh
As Published in 1903

Light on Life's Difficulties
As Published in 1912

Above Life's Turmoil
As Published in 1910

Note from the Editor

Have you ever felt that someone, somewhere, must have understood what you're going through? Have you wondered if some ancient (or not so ancient) master might have some wisdom for you? Have you wished you could understand the writings of the great teachers of the past? If so, then this book is for you.

Here you'll find the essential works of James Allen, who brought the wisdom of the ancients to the modern world. These teachings were offered to initiates in the mystery schools of ancient Egypt and Greece, shared with Christian and pagan mystics through the Renaissance, and rediscovered in the nineteenth century by the poets and philosophers of the Transcendental movement. They are a literary "philosopher's stone," with the power to transform lives.

This is the fifth book in the Library of Hidden Knowledge series, a series that provides modern interpretations of writings from earlier centuries. In this volume we've included Allen's famous *As a Man Thinketh*, one of the most popular self-help books ever written, along with parts of his last book, *Light on Life's Difficulties*, and one that summarized his philosophy, *Above Life's Turmoil*.

Allen wrote these books in southern England during the first decade of the twentieth century—a time when the world was changing rapidly.

Great minds were revolutionizing the realms of thought all over the world, from physics to religion to art, and the Protestant idea of humanity had shifted to suggest that people aren't limited by a sinful nature but, rather, filled with potential for perfection. Writings and teachings from the Eastern religious traditions were newly available in English as well, and Allen used them all—particularly the Buddhist sutras.

His classic *As a Man Thinketh* effectively launched the self-help movement in 1902 and has remained in print ever since, selling thousands of copies each year. The title is based on the verse in Proverbs, which, in the King James version of Allen's time, says "As a man thinketh in his heart so he is" (23:7). The Buddha's famous comment, still used in the Theravada Buddhist canon, "All that we are is the result of what we have thought" was another inspiration.

Allen's book has brought success to millions and is the first selection in this volume. In it, as in all his later books, he made it clear that our lives are a function of the thoughts we've been thinking and the feelings we've felt as a result of those thoughts. So, he wrote, to change our lives we must change our habits of thought. He insisted that each of us has the power to create our own happiness—that we're not "stuck with" the thoughts that float through our minds but can mold them to support our truest desires. Demonstrating that the outer conditions of our life will always be in harmony with our inner state, he detailed how thought leads to action and how to turn our dreams into realities.

Allen went on to write a total of nineteen books in twelve years. In each of them he found new ways to get his message across. When he was done, he had offered the world a new understanding of how our minds work to shape our lives.

The second piece in this volume is a selection from his book *Light on Life's Difficulties*, which we refer to as *Light on Life*. It's not the entire book—just a snippet, the second chapter—but this piece of writing may be Allen's most compelling. It's filled with experience and wisdom. In it, Allen noted that we're not segmented beings but unified; mind, heart, soul, and body are one interconnected whole. He pointed out that confusion and difficulty in life result from playing around with guesses and conjectures, rather than contemplating truths and wisdom. Ultimately, he wrote, "Man is not a being possessing a soul. He himself is soul. He himself is the thinker and doer, actor, and knower." The modern version of this idea, made popular by Wayne Dyer in a number of books, is that we're not physical beings having a spiritual experience; we're spiritual beings having a human experience. Contemplation and meditation based on that fact, Allen wrote, is like turning on a light in a dark room—all confusion ends and we can see where we're going.

The third piece we've included in this volume is his book *Above Life's Turmoil*, which we call *To Rise Above*. It's Allen's invitation for us to experience perfect inner peace regardless of our outer circumstances and thus to transform the outer experience. In the first section he wrote, "Pure happiness is the rightful and healthy condition of the soul, and all may possess it." And the rest of the piece explains how.

Most of us were taught to make things happen by doing things. We were told that if we want to change our environment, we had to get busy and act on it, or move elsewhere. Allen offers a different approach. Our thoughts, he noted, are the basis for our actions: "As the fruit to the tree and the water to the spring, so is action to thought." So for our actions to be effective, we must first pay attention to our thoughts and then change them. Our actions and circumstances will follow.

The exercises at the end of each piece in this book support Allen's philosophy. They are also based on tested processes and have been used in classes and counseling for a decade or more. Many of them suggest a twenty-eight-day cycle of repetition because recent evidence indicates that that is how long it takes to establish a new neural network in the brain.

In all of Allen's works, using his own personal and observed experience, Allen helps us move beyond any limited views of what we can achieve by showing us that our thoughts have unlimited power in the world. Further, he shows us that we need only focus and guide those thoughts to experience our unlimited power and achieve all we've ever dreamed of. This, as he demonstrated in his own life, is not only doable but simple, requiring only our consistent willingness and attention to make it happen.

This philosophy has eased the hearts of people all over the world. It's the basis for Reverend Norman Vincent Peale's *The Power of Positive Thinking* and Reverend Robert Schuller's *Possibility Thinking* as well as Rabbi Joshua Loth Liebman's *Peace of Mind*, and it greatly influenced the popular book and film by Rhonda Byrne, *The Secret*, as well as its sequel, *The Power*.

More than that, modern research, especially in the fields of psychoneuroimmunology and consciousness research, have verified many of his statements. People really are healthier when they focus on what's working in their lives rather than on what disturbs them. People who believe that the world is, as Albert Einstein is reported to have said, "a friendly place," tend to do better than worriers on tests, in school, in sports, and at work. People who choose to feel what we call positive emotions (love, joy, gratitude, and so on) tend to live longer, sleep better, maintain healthier relationships, and have more income at retirement than those who choose to be cynical, skeptical, or fearful.[1]

We're proud to be able to offer James Allen's wonderful compilation of wisdom in the Library of Hidden Knowledge series, and we trust that you will be glad to have discovered the insights Allen offers. As with all of the books in this series, the original texts are printed at the back of the book, following our modernized text, so that you can peruse his words as he wrote them.

May you find here the wisdom to unleash the power of your own thoughts and bring forth a world that gives you only satisfaction, peace, and joy, always!

Ruth L. Miller

As the physically weak man can make himself strong by careful and patient training, so the man of weak thoughts can make them strong by exercising himself in right thinking.

—James Allen
From *As A Man Thinketh* (1903)

ACKNOWLEDGMENTS

Special thanks go to Cindy Black and the staff of Beyond Words for conceiving this project and for making it easy to bring these insightful and useful ideas into the modern world. Particular appreciation goes to Henry Covey for making the first-cut version and asking all the right questions.

INTRODUCTION

James Allen was born in Leicester, England, on November 28, 1864. His working-class family included his two younger brothers, his mother, who could neither read nor write, and his father, who worked in a factory operating a knitting machine for a living. Theirs was a comfortable life, if poor and uneventful. There was no hint in those early years of the upcoming events that would usher the young Allen into a world of prosperity thinkers. There was no sign that he would ultimately develop a prolific writing career that would launch a new movement, changing the way people everywhere see and perceive themselves today.

Growing Up Fast

In the late 1870s, when Allen was still a young boy, the textile trade of central England dropped into severe depression. To find work and establish a new home for the family, his father William took what little money they had and traveled to America. Like most men in that position, he intended to send for the rest of the family later.

Sadly, tragedy struck almost immediately. Within two days of William's arrival, he was pronounced dead at New York City Hospital, believed to be the victim of robbery and murder. (This period is illustrated in the Martin Scorsese film *Gangs of New York*.) An empty pocketbook and an old silver watch were the only items found on his body.

So, at age fifteen, James was forced to drop out of school and find work to support his mother and two younger brothers. He started out as a common laborer in a local textile factory, working the same type of stocking-frame knitting machine that his father had operated before him, but Allen's ability to write and organize his ideas caught the attention of the factory's owner, who made Allen his private secretary.

This was a whole new world—a world based on thought rather than labor—and the young James Allen blossomed in it. Although he worked long hours at the office to help keep the family afloat (a workweek was six days, ten hours a day), he still found time to read and study. In fact, he turned out to be a real literary animal and, around the age of seventeen, he discovered Shakespeare, his first literary love: "I read Shakespeare in the early morning, at breakfast time, in the dinner hour, and in the evening," he was once quoted as saying.[1]

Then he discovered Ralph Waldo Emerson, an American writer whose transcendentalist prose lifted Allen into a higher realm of mind than he'd experienced in the dramas based on pain and suffering in Shakespeare's fiery passions and fleeting pleasures. He was deeply impressed by the essays "Compensation" and "The Over-Soul," but it was in the essay "Self Reliance" that he found the idea that worth and dignity are a potential in everyone's character—to be developed through carefully considered thought and action. We see glimmers of Emerson's style throughout Allen's works later on.

Emerson's writings also introduced Allen to the poetry and literature of the East, which captured Allen's imagination and opened up new spiritual possibilities. At about the age of twenty-four, Allen read *The Light of Asia* by Sir Edwin Arnold, an epic poem about an imaginary Buddhist monk who symbolizes the life, character, and philosophy of Prince Gautama of India, the founder of Buddhism. Of all the works of poetry he absorbed in those early years, from Whitman to Milton, it was Sir Arnold's that led to Allen's spiritual metamorphosis. Describing his experience the first time he read *Light of Asia*, Allen wrote,

I could not stir from my seat till I read every word. When I did rise from the reading of this book, it was as though I had become a different man. A curtain seemed to have rolled back from the face of the Universe, and I saw the causes and meaning of things which had hitherto been dark mysteries. There was a revelation which was almost blinding in its brilliance and suddenness, an exaltation which alarmed me while it transported me into a felicitous insight. The vision quickly faded, but its influence remained, the memory of it saving me in many an hour of darkness and temptation.[2]

A "different man," Allen continued his journey into the literary realms of Eastern thought. By the age of twenty-six he had devoured the Bhagavad Gita, the Tao Te Ching, various books by Chinese sages like Confucius, as well as *The Gospel of Buddha*, by Paul Carus, and Dr. Richard M. Bucke's *Cosmic Consciousness: A Study in the Evolution of the Human Mind*.

Finding His Voice

In 1893 the ambitious and now-empowered Allen moved to London for a new job, and soon a new life started falling into place. He met Lily Louisa Oram, and they married in 1895. Their daughter, Nora, was born the following year, and a year after that, Allen began to work for a magazine called *The Herald of the Golden Age*, supplementing his income and developing his writing and editing skills as well as his spiritual and social interests.[3]

After a couple of years with *The Herald*, Allen had learned what he needed and collected enough material to write and publish the first of many books, *From Poverty to Power* (1901). This book was so well received that just a year later, in 1902, Allen broke away from *The Herald* and launched his own spiritual magazine, *The Light of Reason*. Each issue of *The Light* contained announcements, an editorial written by Allen, and many articles, poems, and quotes by popular authors of the day and even local unknown authors.

Later that same year Allen published his most famous work, *As a Man Thinketh*. It was a mouse of a book that roared around the world, solidifying Allen's place as one of the pioneering figures of modern inspirational thought. Allen is said to have been at first dissatisfied with the book, even though it most concisely embodied his thought. His wife was the one to recognize its value and persuaded him to publish it.

With the success of *As a Man Thinketh*, Allen started earning enough to allow him to leave the urban world of business and move his work and family to the quiet Victorian seaside town of Ilfracombe, England. There the Allens would live for the next decade in a small home called *Bryngoleu* (a Welsh term meaning "Hill of Light") located on a winding lane nestled against the picturesque green hillsides overlooking the Celtic Sea. It was in this scenic, peaceful place that Allen wrote most of his letters, books, and articles, far from the cramped urban jungle of his working-class childhood in Leicester.

Living the Light

Allen's day in Ilfracombe began with a predawn walk to the Cairn, a locally famous pile of stones on the hillside overlooking his home and the sea. There he would remain for an hour or so in meditation. Then he would return to the house and spend the morning working on something for his magazine or writing one of his many books. Afternoons were devoted mostly to gardening, a pastime he enjoyed and, like Emerson, one he believed was part of a healthy life. His evenings were spent in conversation with the many people who came to visit because they were interested in his work.

Bryngoleu was the perfect environment for Allen, and it was here that his writing really took off. His books and the magazine were reaching readers throughout the world, in America, Australia, New Zealand, and India. Letters poured in from all over; they came in so fast that, for a short time Allen produced nothing but responses to these requests for information and support.

In an effort to meet this growing interest, Allen established the Brotherhood, which was also called the School of Virtue, in 1905.

The central doctrine of the Brotherhood is what we call Oneness in the adapted text: the practice of unconditional love toward all beings through the renunciation of the small, egoic self for the good of the world. Groups met regularly in various countries, and a report of their meetings was printed each month in Allen's magazine under the heading "Our Groups and Their Work." Allen and his wife often traveled to group meetings to give talks and read articles.

People came from around the world—England, France, Austria, and India—to visit the Allens at Bryngoleu, so the Allens ran their home as a salon of intellectuals, where they would talk with their guests late into the evening on topics ranging from meditation and philosophy to the life and ideas of Tolstoy or Buddha.

A Literary Legacy

Allen stayed in Ilfracombe, writing for the magazine and producing one or two books per year until his death at the age of forty-seven years in 1912. He had written a total of nineteen books in all, some of which his wife published after he had passed on.

The exact cause of Allen's death is not known, but we do know that his body was cremated. His brother Thomas, who was also a writer and sometimes contributor to Allen's monthly journal, scattered his brother's ashes in the cemetery surrounding the crematorium with a blessing:

> As these ashes of James Allen are cast to the four winds of Heaven, so may the Truth he taught permeate to the four corners of the earth, carrying with it Joy, Peace, and Consolation.[4]

There was no formal funeral. Survived by his wife and their daughter, Allen left everything to Lily and named her and Thomas executors of his estate.

Allen seems to have died a happy man. He never became rich in the material sense, but the wealth he sought was beyond measure. He believed that we become spiritually rich when we discover the power within—when we are conscious of the Oneness of all life; when we practice discernment, self-discipline, and meditation; and when we experience kinship with others and with nature. Then, he found, all that we ever need or desire is available to us.

Lily continued spreading her husband's works, and published their magazine under the name *The Epoch* for several more years. She continued to run Bryngoleu as a guesthouse and also wrote books of her own. She summarized her husband's literary mission in the preface to one of these books, *Foundation Stones to Happiness and Success*:

> He never wrote theories, or for the sake of writing; but he wrote when he had a message, and it became a message only when he had lived it out in his own life, and knew that it was good. Thus he wrote facts, which he had proven by practice.[5]

A small, reserved man with unruly, flowing black hair and gentle eyes, Allen made a lasting impression on people he encountered. He had a gentle nature and, with the Hindu/Buddhist concept of reverence for life, advocated killing nothing, not even a mouse in the garden.

He strove to live the life that the Essenes of Jesus's time had advocated and that Leo Tolstoy and later Mohandas K. Gandhi encouraged: a life of voluntary simplicity, with daily manual labor and ongoing management of the mind. Though raised Methodist, he drew inspiration from many religions and influenced the leaders of the Church of England (the Anglican/Episcopalian denomination) in a way that was made visible in the works of his great friend Archdeacon Wilberforce. Like Tolstoy, Benjamin Franklin, and the great teachers before them, Allen always sought to improve himself, to rid his thought and action of anything harmful, to embody all that was good and true, and to be happy. He once wrote,

> Confucius said, "The perfecting of one's self is the fundamental base of all progress and of all moral development." A maxim as profound and comprehensive as it is simple and

practical, and uninvolved, for there is no surer way to knowledge, nor better way to help the world than by perfecting one's self. Nor is there any nobler work or higher science than that of self-perfection.[6]

Allen generally disliked publicity, and it may be because of his disregard for flashy advertisement that he's not as well-known as some. But his many books are a monument to his memory. He was strong, true, and individual, a man who wrote and spoke out of the depth of his own convictions—an intellectual who thought from the heart.

Modernizing James Allen's Language

As a British author writing at the turn of the twentieth century, James Allen used the flowery prose of his age. On top of that, many of his words no longer exist in common use or their meanings have been lost or changed over the years.

The most obvious change made to this modern adaptation is demonstrated in the title of the first piece, *As We Think*, which we changed from *As a Man Thinketh*. Of course, Allen's gender-specific language was just a part of the writing style back then. When we look deeper, we realize that Allen's message applies to all women and men and to people of all walks of life and levels of consciousness.

Yet, as distracting as his original style can be at times, the real gems of Allen's philosophy and method are still powerfully presented in his masterful prose. He had a special way of turning a phrase and distilling truth that makes you think in a new way at first and then you immediately see the wisdom. Like Emerson, he was a philosopher-poet who wrote in a direct and universal style that expressed his thoughts powerfully and gave his work a special niche.

His was the perfect voice for a whole new movement of thought in a world headed toward the Atomic Age. There are times when his words sometimes eerily match the wisdom or happenings of today, as if what he's talking about has been ripped from the headlines. For example, in *Light on Life*, he wrote,

The world is in a condition of mental ferment. Contradiction has reached the point of confusion, so that the earnest seeker for Truth can find no solid rock of refuge in the opposing systems which are presented.

These words applied in his day and are compelling in our world today. This was his reason for writing—to help everyone, everywhere, to be freed from undue stress and worry.

When we look at what Allen said about the power of the mind and the impact of thoughts, we also find that it's directly in line with modern discoveries in neurology. Through the use of brain scans, it's been shown that when a thought is produced and repeated; it literally grows and strengthens new neural pathways, which, over time, lead to a new filter for interpreting our perceptions.

Allen also showed the connection between the mind and the body. In *As We Think*, he wrote,

Sickly thoughts express themselves through a sickly body. Fear has been known to kill a person as speedily as a bullet, and fearful thoughts are continually killing thousands of people just as surely, though less rapidly. The people who live in fear of disease are the people who get it. Anxiety compromises and weakens the body, and lays it open to the entrance of disease; while fearful, attacking, or lustful thoughts, even if not physically indulged, will soon shatter the nervous system.

These words read like a description of psychosomatics and could be part of the definition of the developing field of psychoneuroimmunology. In essence, science and medicine are only now establishing the experimental validity of what he understood philosophically more than a century ago.

When we finally work our way through all the antiquated language, Allen's words lead us through the realms of political and social behavior, neurology, and physiology. His works distill the essential teachings of the ancient schools and bring them into the early twentieth century. He made those teachings his own and shared them from his personal experience, using a poet's skill to bring his points clearly home.

We've made every attempt to honor his particular style while bringing his language into modern usage. We hope that these adaptations will bring his amazing wisdom into the twenty-first century. We hope you enjoy them and find them as useful as so many have before.

How to Use This Book

This book includes three of Allen's works. To help you keep track of their respective philosophies, each chapter in the first part—the "Interpretations"—closes with a summary of essential points, along with any notes on the text. And each of the three books ends with exercises you can use immediately to start implementing Allen's methods with tangible and practical spiritual results.

As with all the books in the Library of Hidden Knowledge series, the author's original version of the texts appears at the back of the book. For the most powerful experience, we recommend that you look over the whole book first, taking in what leaps off the page, wherever it appears. Then go through the first chapter, the adaptation titled *As We Think*. Read it and try the exercise at the end. Then take a look at Allen's original text in the second part of the book, *As a Man Thinketh*. You will find the original text much easier to read, and you may even find that there's a particular phrase or description of Allen's that brings an idea into clearer focus. Do the same for each section of the book, *Light on Life* and *To Rise Above*, following up with its original in the back.

Used this way, this book will help you experience a greater, more satisfactory sense of self, a new power to achieve any worthwhile personal purpose, and a new ability to enjoy life's beauty and wonder.

• • •

I dreamed of writing books which would help men and women, whether rich or poor, learned or unlearned, worldly or unworldly to find within themselves the source of all success, all happiness, accomplishment, all truth. And the dream remained with me, and at last became substantial; and now I send forth these books into the world on a mission of healing and blessedness, knowing that they cannot fail to reach the homes and hearts of those who are waiting and ready to receive them . . . who are eager to learn, and earnest to achieve . . . who will put away (for the world's good) a petty personal indulgence, a selfish desire, a mean thought, . . . without craving and regret.[7]

James Allen

INTERPRETATIONS

MODERNIZED FOR THE
TWENTY-FIRST-CENTURY READER

As We Think

Mind is the master power that molds and makes,
And we are mind, and evermore we take
The tool of thought, and, shaping what we will,
Bring forth a thousand joys, a thousand ills—
We think in secret, and it comes to pass:
Environment is but our looking glass.

—James Allen

Introduction: We Make Ourselves

This brief overview, the result of meditation and experience, is not intended as an exhaustive explanation of the power of thought. Its purpose is not to explain but to inspire humanity to the discovery and understanding of this truth:

We are the makers of ourselves by virtue of the thoughts
we choose and encourage;

Mind is the master weaver of both the inner garment of character
and the outer garment of circumstance;

And as we may have until now woven in ignorance and pain,
we may now weave in enlightenment and happiness.

James Allen

1

THOUGHT AND CHARACTER

The idea "As we think in our hearts, so we are" not only embraces our whole being but reaches out to all our conditions and circumstances. We literally are what we think and our lives are the product of our thoughts.

As the plant springs from the seed—and could not exist without it—so every one of our actions springs from the hidden seeds of our thoughts and could not have appeared without them. Even those actions that we call "spontaneous" and "unpremeditated"—as well as those we've carefully and intentionally executed—are, and can only be, products of our thought.

And if action is the flower of thought, then joy and suffering are its fruits. We reap the sweet and bitter fruit that we sow, because what we've become was built with our thoughts. If our thoughts are fearful and hateful, trouble and distress will cloud our paths, but if our thoughts are peaceful and loving, focused on the higher Truth, bliss and blessedness follow us as surely as our shadows follow us on a sunny day.

We either make or unmake ourselves; we either forge the weapons that destroy us or make the tools to build heavenly mansions of joy, strength, and peace. With considered choice and the application of true thought, we ascend to divine perfection, while by the abuse and unprincipled application of thought, we descend below the level of animals. Between these two extremes are all the grades of character, and we are their makers and rulers.

We develop, therefore, by the natural laws of cause and effect, and these laws are as absolute and unchanging in the hidden realm of thought as they are in the world of visible and material things. If someone is gracious and godlike, it's not because they're favored or lucky; it's the natural result of their continued compassionate thinking, the effect of their long-cherished focus on high principles and godly qualities. Similarly, if someone is mean and coarse, it's the result of their continued dwelling on mean and coarse thoughts.

Of all the beautiful truths that have been restored and brought to light in this age, none will promise you more joy and blessedness in mind and spirit than this—that you are the master of your thoughts, the molder of your character, and the maker and shaper of your condition, your environment, and your destiny. As a being of power, intelligence, and love and the controller of your own thoughts, you hold the key to every situation; you contain within yourself all the means to make yourself and your life what you will.

We're always in charge of our thoughts and actions, even in our weakest and most abandoned states, when we sometimes think and act foolishly. But when we can reflect on our condition and search diligently for the laws of cause and effect that govern our being, it's possible to discover them within ourselves. Then we become wise, directing our energies with intelligence and managing our thoughts for desired results.

This discovery is absolutely the result of attention, self-analysis, and experience. As gold and diamonds are obtained through much searching and mining, we can find every truth contained within our being if we're willing to dig deep into the mine of our own minds.

We watch, control, and change our thoughts, tracing their effects in our lives and circumstances. Then we link cause and effect by patient practice and investigation, considering all our experiences, even the most trivial, as a way to gain knowledge of our self. This is the only way that the absolute law—"Everyone who asks receives, and the one who seeks finds, and to the one who knocks it will be opened" (Matthew 7:7–8)—works. For only with patience, practice, and persistence can the door to the temple of knowledge be unlocked.

Essential Points

- Every one of our actions springs from the hidden seeds of thought and could not have appeared without them.
- We are the masters of our thoughts, the molders of our character, and the makers and shapers of our condition.
- As beings of power, intelligence, and love and the controllers of our own thoughts, we hold the key to every situation.
- We can find every truth contained within our being if we're willing to dig deep into the mine of our own minds.

2

THE EFFECT OF THOUGHT
ON CIRCUMSTANCES

We can describe the mind as a garden that may be carefully cultivated or allowed to run wild. Whether cultivated or neglected,
however, it must grow—and it will. If no useful seeds are planted, then
useless weeds will grow instead of the desired flowers and fruits, and
they will continue to intrude and produce their kind.

Just as gardeners cultivate their garden plots, keeping them free
from weeds and growing the flowers and fruits they require for sustenance, we can tend the gardens of our minds. We do this by weeding
out all the harmful, useless, and unhealthy thoughts and cultivating
the flowers and fruits of good, useful, and loving thoughts. It is our
decision: we are the master gardeners of our minds, the directors of
our lives.

Thinking of the mind as a garden helps us understand how the
forces and elements of the mind work to shape character, circumstances,
and destiny. Everyone is where they are by the law of their being; there's
no element of chance in the arrangement of our lives—it's all the result
of natural law.

The thoughts you've built into your character have brought you to
where you are today, for thought and character are one. And the outer
conditions of your life will always harmoniously reflect your inner state,

since everyone's character is manifest and discovered through his or her environment and circumstance.

This doesn't mean that circumstances at any given time provide a full image of someone's entire character. It means, instead, that our current circumstances are so intimately connected with some vital element of recent thought patterns that the circumstances of the moment are essential for our development.

This is just as true for those who feel "out of harmony" with their surroundings as for those who are content with them. We're only distressed by circumstances as long as we believe ourselves to be creatures of outside conditions. But when we realize that we command the hidden soil and seeds out of which our circumstances grow, we become the rightful rulers of ourselves and our situations.

Those who have managed their thoughts and actions for any length of time know this truth. They can see changes in their environment in direct proportion to the changes in their mental condition. Once they start to seriously release and replace the thoughts and beliefs that no longer serve them, they go through a rapid series of changes in their lives.

This is because people don't attract what they want but they attract what they are. Their whims, fancies, and ambitions may be thwarted at every step or may be attained, but their innermost thoughts and desires manifest daily. We don't get what we wish and pray for but what we earn by the focus of our thoughts. Our wishes and prayers are only gratified and answered when they harmonize with our thoughts and actions.

We all reach the height of our highest hopes and fall to the level of our lowliest thoughts in the world, for our circumstances are the means by which we receive our own. And this is because we each attract what we secretly hold true—what we love as well as what we fear.

Every seed of thought that's sown or allowed to fall into the mind and take root blossoms sooner or later into action, bearing its own fruit in opportunity and circumstance—good thoughts bearing good fruit, and bad thoughts producing bad fruit. For example, people don't end up in the poorhouse or jail by fate or circumstance but by their own lowly thoughts and base desires. Nor does a normally principled person fall suddenly into crime by external force; the criminal thought has to be secretly fostered in the heart for some time before the hour of opportunity can reveal its power. Descending into vice and its consequent sufferings can't happen without vicious inclinations in the mind, while ascending into pure happiness can't happen without continually cultivating worthy aspirations.

So we see that circumstances don't make us; in fact, they reveal us to ourselves. Good thoughts and actions can never produce bad results; bad thoughts and actions can never produce good results. This is simply saying that nothing can come from corn but corn and nothing from nettle seeds but nettles. It's a law in the natural world, and we're best served to work with it in the mental and moral world, though few understand how it applies and therefore don't benefit from it.

Aware that we're the reapers of our own harvests, though, we learn from both suffering and bliss. As improving and evolving beings, we are where we are so that we may learn and grow, and as we learn the spiritual lesson that any situation holds for us, the situation passes away, leaving room for other circumstances. So both pleasant and unpleasant external conditions are factors leading to our ultimate good.

The "divinity that shapes our ends," then, is the collection of healthy and unhealthy thoughts within ourselves—our very self. Thought and action can be both the jailers of fate and the angels of freedom. If they're low-minded or hostile, they imprison; if they're high-minded and just, they liberate. Ultimately, we decide whether or not to handcuff ourselves to our own selves.

As the controllers and rulers of our thoughts, therefore, we are the makers of ourselves, the shapers and authors of our environments and destinies—from birth, when the soul comes into form, and through every step of our lives on earth. The soul that we are attracts those combinations of conditions that reveal it, that reflect its own clarity and toxicity, strength and weakness.

The circumstances we encounter with suffering are always the result of our own mental discord, while the circumstances we appreciate and bless are the measure of our continuing appreciative and praise-filled thoughts. Given this truth, why would we fight against circumstances? Most of us are continually rebelling against an effect that we ourselves have created, even while we're nourishing and preserving its cause in our hearts. That cause may take the form of a conscious choice or an unconscious weakness; but whatever it is, it makes our lives less than they could be, and so calls for remedy.

Applying the Laws of Thought

Most people are anxious to improve their circumstances, but many are unwilling to improve themselves—and remain imprisoned as a result. By contrast, those who don't shrink from overcoming the lesser self can never fail to accomplish their heart's intention. This is as true for worldly things as it is for heavenly ones. Even if your sole object is to acquire wealth, you must be prepared to make great personal sacrifices, to let go of unproductive patterns of thinking and habits of acting, before you can accomplish your objective.

Consider people who are poor and want very much to improve their surroundings and home comforts yet shirk their work, considering themselves justified in trying to deceive their employers because of their low wages. These people don't understand the simplest principles of true prosperity. They're not only totally unfit to rise out of their poor conditions but are actually attracting to themselves still deeper wretchedness by dwelling in—and acting out—lazy, deceptive, and cowardly thoughts.

Consider wealthy folk who are the victims of a painful and persistent disease as the result of gluttony. They would pay lots of money to get rid of their disease yet will not sacrifice their gluttonous desires. They may have money but have not yet learned the first principles of a healthy life. They can't continue indulging in large quantities of rich and unnatural foods and have good health, too.

We can also consider CEOs who avoid paying living wages, and in the hope of making still larger profits, reduce their workers' benefits or stockholders' dividends. Such people are altogether unfit for prosperity.

And when they find themselves bankrupt in both reputation and riches, they blame the circumstances, not understanding that they've been the sole authors of their condition.

These three cases merely illustrate the truth that people are the cause (though nearly always unknowingly) of their circumstances. That, while aiming for a desirable end, they continually frustrate its accomplishment by encouraging thoughts and desires that can't possibly harmonize with that end. Such cases could be multiplied and varied almost indefinitely, but it's not necessary.

Each of us can trace the action of the laws of thought in our own minds and lives, but we can't usually see them at work until we've done so. And no one can do it for us. Individual circumstances are so complicated, thought is so deeply rooted, and the conditions of happiness vary so greatly that no one's entire condition (although it may be known to that individual) can be judged by anyone outside.

For example, one person may be generally honest yet still suffer hardship. Another may often be dishonest yet acquire wealth. The usual assumption that one fails because of honesty and the other prospers because of dishonesty is the result of an underlying belief that dishonest people are almost totally corrupt, while honest people are almost entirely virtuous. But with deeper knowledge and wider experience, this assumption is shown to be baseless. The dishonest person may have some virtues that the other lacks, while the honest one may hide vices that the other abhors. The honest reap the good results of their honest thoughts and actions as well as the sufferings their vices produce. The dishonest likewise reap their own mixture of suffering and happiness.

It's normal in our culture to think that people suffer because they're virtuous. But only if we've completely uprooted every sickly, bitter, and fearful thought from our minds and washed every stain of the past from our souls can we know and declare that our suffering is the result of our good qualities. And as we do so, we will find the great Law working in our minds and lives. That Law is absolutely just and cannot give good for evil or evil for good, so we'll know, looking back upon our past ignorance and blindness, that all our past experiences, good and bad, were simply the reflection of our evolving but not yet evolved self.

In fact, any form of suffering is always the effect of misguided thought. It's an indication that we're out of harmony with ourselves and with the Law of our being. The sole and supreme use of suffering is to burn out whatever is useless and toxic in our thoughts and memories. Suffering ceases for those who are perfectly clear and enlightened; after all, there's no point in burning gold after the impurities have been removed.

Misery, not lack of material possessions, is therefore the best measure of misguided thought. Misery has two extremes: destitution and indulgence. They're equally unnatural, and both are the result of disordered thinking. In general, people may be either miserable and rich or blessed and poor. The rich are only blessed when the riches are lovingly and wisely used, and the poor only descend into misery when they regard their lack of riches as a burden.

We can be sure we're not in our right minds until we're happy, healthy, and prosperous. And happiness, health, and prosperity are the result of a harmonious relationship between our happy, healthy, prosperous thoughts and our surroundings. They come when the whining and criticizing stop and the search for the hidden process that regulates life begins. Then, as we adapt our minds to that regulator, we begin to stop blaming others for our conditions and build ourselves up with strong and principled thoughts. We cease to kick against circumstances and begin to use them as aids to more rapid progress, helping us discover the hidden powers and possibilities within ourselves.

Powers and Possibilities of Thought

Order, not confusion, is the dominating principle in the universe. Justice, not injustice, is the essence and substance of life. And uprightness, not corruption, is the molding and moving force in the spiritual government of the world.

This being so, we have but to set ourselves right to find that the universe is right. In the process of establishing ourselves in harmonious alignment with the universal principle, we find that the world of our experience has changed. We see that as we change our thoughts about things and other people, those things and other people change in their attitudes and behaviors toward us.

So while we cannot directly choose our circumstances, we can choose our thoughts and therefore, indirectly yet surely, shape our circumstances. And when we radically shift our thoughts, we experience a rapid transformation in the material conditions of our lives. When we cease having cynical and fearful thoughts, the whole world softens toward us and is ready to help. When we put away weak and sickly thoughts, lo and behold, opportunities spring up everywhere to aid our new strong resolve. When we encourage good thoughts, no hard fate could ever bind us to distress and shame.

Some imagine that thought can be kept secret, but it can't. Thought rapidly crystallizes into habit, and habit solidifies into circumstance, either blessed or miserable. Specifically,

- Fearful and misguided thoughts of every kind crystallize into debilitating and confusing habits, which solidify into distracting and adverse circumstances.
- Habits of drunkenness and sensuality solidify into circumstances of destitution and disease.
- Thoughts of fear, doubt, and indecision crystallize into weak, dishonorable, and indecisive habits, which solidify into circumstances of failure, indigence, and slavish dependence.
- Lazy thoughts crystallize into habits of disorder and dishonesty, which solidify into circumstances of foulness and destitution.
- Hostile and critical thoughts crystallize into habits of accusation and violence, which solidify into circumstances of injury and persecution.
- Selfish thoughts of all kinds crystallize into habits of self-seeking, which solidify into distressing circumstances of all kinds.

On the other hand, when we place our focus on our highest dreams and ideals, our life falls into alignment with them:

- Beautiful thoughts crystallize into habits of grace and kindness, which solidify into genial and sunny circumstances.
- Noble thoughts crystallize into habits of temperance and self-control, which solidify into circumstances of peace and rest.
- Thoughts of courage, self-reliance, and decision crystallize into strong and constructive habits, which solidify into circumstances of success, plenty, and freedom.
- Energetic thoughts crystallize into habits of cleanliness and effectiveness, which solidify into circumstances of pleasantness.
- Gentle and forgiving thoughts crystallize into habits of gentleness, which solidify into safe and healthy circumstances.
- Loving and unselfish thoughts crystallize into habits of doing good for others, which solidify into circumstances of sure and abiding prosperity and true riches.

The proof of these truths is in everyone. As William H. Murray and Ralph Waldo Emerson remind us, Nature helps everyone fulfill the thoughts that are most encouraged under its laws. The universe is constantly presenting us with opportunities that will most speedily bring both good and harmful thoughts to the surface of our awareness.[1] From there, it is up to us to choose which thoughts receive our energy.

The world is your personal kaleidoscope, and the ever-changing combinations of colors it presents are the exquisitely adjusted pictures of your ever-moving thoughts.

You will be what you will to be;
Let failure find its false content
In that poor word, "environment,"
But spirit scorns it and is free.

It masters time, it conquers space;
It cows that boastful trickster, Chance,
And bids the tyrant Circumstance
Uncrown and fill a servant's place.

The human Will, that force unseen,
The offspring of a deathless Soul,
Can hew a way to any goal,
Though walls of granite intervene.

Be not impatient in delay,
But wait as one who understands;
When spirit rises and commands,
The gods are ready to obey.[2]

Essential Points

- Just as gardeners keep their plots free from weeds to grow the flowers and fruits they require for sustenance, we tend the gardens of our minds, weeding out all the useless and unhealthy thoughts and cultivating the flowers and fruits of noble, useful, and loving thoughts.
- Each of us attracts what we secretly hold true—what we love as well as what we fear.
- Happiness, health, and prosperity only come when the whining and criticizing stop and the search for the hidden balance that regulates all life is begun.
- The outer conditions of our lives always reflect our inner states, so circumstances don't make us; they reveal us to ourselves.
- As we change our thoughts about things and other people, those things and other people change in their attitudes and behaviors toward us.

3

THE EFFECT OF THOUGHT ON HEALTH AND THE BODY

The body is the servant of the mind. As Candace Pert, microbiologist and author of *Molecules of Emotion*, tells us in the film *What the BLEEP Do We Know!?*, the body is the unconscious mind. All our emotional memories and responses are stored in and around our cells. Medical intuitive Carolyn Myss, in her book *Anatomy of Spirit*, explains this idea, saying that our biology is our biography.

The body obeys the operations of the mind, whether they're deliberately chosen or automatically expressed. Disease and health, like circumstances, are rooted in thought. Doctors have long known that any treatment that the patient believes will be effective will lead to improvement in 25 to 40 percent of cases through a process called the placebo effect.

This is just an example of the fact that the body is a delicate and moldable instrument that responds readily to the thoughts that impress it. And habits of thought, good or bad, will affect it. Sickly thoughts express themselves through a sickly body. Fear has been known to kill a person as speedily as a bullet, and fearful thoughts are continually killing thousands of people just as surely, though less rapidly. The people who live in fear of disease are the people who get it. Anxiety compromises and weakens the body and lays it open to disease, while fearful, attacking, or lustful thoughts, even if not actually indulged, will shatter the nervous system.

People will continue to have toxic and poisoned systems as long as they focus on toxic thoughts, whereas strong, loving, and happy thoughts build up the body in vigor and grace. A change of diet won't help those who refuse to change their thoughts. In fact, it works the other way around: when we make our thoughts healthy, we no longer desire unhealthy food. Out of a clean "heart," or emotional mind, comes a clean life and a clean body. Out of a polluted mind proceeds a defiled life and corrupt body.

Thought is the fountain of action, life, and manifestation. Make the fountain clear and all will be clear. If you plan on perfecting your body, guard your mind. If you intend to renew your body, beautify your mind. Thoughts of hostility, envy, disappointment, or despondency rob the body of its health and grace.

With thoughts of discord and distress, the body sinks rapidly into disease and decay, while at the command of glad and beautiful thoughts, it becomes clothed with youth and beauty. We see this in our own lives simply by looking in the mirror on the days when we feel great and on the days we wish we didn't have to get up.

A sour face does not come by chance; it's made by sour thoughts. Unsightly wrinkles are drawn by folly, self-justification, and pride. I know a woman of ninety-six who has the bright, innocent face of a girl. I also know a man well under middle age whose face is badly mis-shapen and wrinkled. One is the result of a sweet and sunny disposition; the other is the outcome of complaints and discontent. Just as you can't have a sweet and wholesome home unless you let air and sunshine freely into your rooms, so a strong body and a bright, happy, or serene face can only result from letting thoughts of joy, goodwill, and serenity into the mind.

There are wrinkles on the faces of the aged made by sympathy; others are carved by intensely determined thought; still others by untamed passion. Who can't see the difference? For those who have lived harmoniously, age is calm, peaceful, and softly mellowed, like the setting sun. I have recently seen a philosopher on his deathbed. He was not old except in years and died as sweetly and peacefully as he had lived.

As Norman Cousins discovered and described in his book *Anatomy of an Illness as Perceived by the Patient*, there's no physician like cheerful thought for healing the ills of the body, and there's no comforter that can compare with goodwill for dispersing the shadows of grief and sorrow. To live continually in thoughts of ill will, cynicism, suspicion, or envy is to be confined in a self-made prison. But to think well of all, to be cheerful with all, to patiently learn to find the good in all—such unselfish thoughts are the portals to heaven; and to maintain daily thoughts of peace toward every creature will bring abounding peace to one's life.

Essential Points

- Disease and health, like circumstances, are rooted in thought.
- With thoughts of discord and distress, the body sinks rapidly into disease and decay; at the command of glad and beautiful thoughts, the body is healthy, vigorous, and beautiful.
- A strong body and a bright and happy or serene face can only result from letting thoughts of joy, goodwill, and serenity into the mind.
- There's no physician like cheerful thought for healing the ills of the body.

4

THOUGHT AND PURPOSE

With most people, the ship of thought is allowed to drift upon the ocean of life, but such drifting must not continue for those who would steer clear of catastrophe and destruction. People who have no central purpose in their life fall easy prey to worries, fears, troubles, and self-pity, all of which are indications of weakness and lead to failure, unhappiness, and loss. Such weakness cannot persist in an ever-increasing, evolving universe, and until thought is linked with purpose, there is no intelligent accomplishment.

Applying the Laws of Thought

Fortunately, just as the physically weak can make themselves strong by careful and patient training, those with weak thoughts can make themselves strong by exercising focused thought. Even the weakest soul, knowing its own weakness and believing the truth that strength can only be developed by effort and practice, will at once begin to exert itself. Then, adding effort to effort, patience to patience, and strength to strength, this soul will never cease to develop and will at last grow divinely strong.

To put away aimlessness and weakness and begin to think with purpose is to enter the ranks of the strong. In doing so, we join the ranks of people who learn from their failures, who make all conditions serve them, and who think powerfully, attempt fearlessly, and accomplish masterfully.

The strong cannot help the weak unless the weak are willing to be helped, and even then the weak must become stronger themselves. They must, by their own endeavors, develop the strength they admire in someone else. Only then can they alter their condition.

Some say, "Many are slaves because one is an oppressor; therefore, we should hate the oppressor." Others reverse this judgment and say, "One is an oppressor because many are slaves; we should despise the slaves." The truth is that the oppressor and the slaves are cooperators in ignorance, and, while seeming to afflict each other, both are in reality afflicting themselves.

A perfect knowledge perceives the action of law
in the weakness of the oppressed
and the misapplied power of the oppressor;

A perfect love, seeing the suffering that both states entail, condemns neither;
and a perfect compassion embraces both oppressor and oppressed.

Those who have conquered inner weakness and put away all selfish thoughts belong neither to oppressor nor oppressed. They are free.

Essential Points

- Just as the physically weak can make themselves strong by careful and patient training, so can those with weak thoughts make themselves strong by exercising focused thought.
- The strong cannot help the weak unless the weak are willing to be helped, and even then the weak must become strong themselves, for only they can alter their condition.
- Those who have conquered inner weakness and put away all selfish thoughts belong neither to oppressor nor oppressed. They are free.

5

THE ROLE OF THOUGHT
IN ACHIEVEMENT

All that we achieve and all that we fail to achieve is the direct result of our own thoughts. Our weaknesses and strengths, clarities and faults, are our own and not anyone else's. We are their cause, no one else, and they can only be altered by us, never by others. Our conditions are also our own and not anyone else's. Our suffering and our happiness evolve from within. This is because in a justly ordered universe, balance is always maintained; loss of balance in any part would mean total destruction, so individual responsibility for individual experience must be absolute.

As you think, so you are; as you continue to think,
so you remain.

Barriers to Achievement

The will to act springs from the knowledge that we can act. Doubt and fear are the great enemies of that knowledge, and those who encourage such thoughts and don't cancel them immediately are just getting in their own way. Doubt and fear should be rigorously banned from every endeavor; they break up the solid, straight line of endeavor, rendering it crooked, ineffectual, and useless. They never can accomplish anything.

Doubt always leads to failure. Purpose, energy, the power to act and create, and all other strong thoughts die when either doubt or fear creeps in.

But those who have conquered doubt and fear have conquered failure. Their every thought is allied with power, and all difficulties are bravely met and wisely overcome. Their purposes are planted in season, and they bloom and bring forth fruit that can't fall prematurely and rot.

The desire for immediate gratification is just as useless. Those whose first thought is how to indulge their immediate desires can neither think clearly nor plan methodically. They can't find and develop their latent resources and so fail in their undertakings. This failure to effectively control their thoughts means they're in no position to control projects or organizations or to adopt any serious responsibilities. They aren't fit to act independently and stand alone, being limited by the thoughts they choose. So before we can achieve anything, even in worldly things, we must lift our thoughts above slavish self-indulgence. We don't have to give up all selfishness in order to succeed, by any means, but a portion of it must at least be released.

This is because the universe doesn't favor the greedy, the dishonest, or the vicious, although on the surface it may sometimes seem like it does. Structured to support the soul's fulfillment, the universe helps the honest, the magnanimous, the loving. All the great spiritual teachers of the ages have declared this in different ways, and we have only to become more honest, magnanimous, and loving to prove it for ourselves. The higher we lift our thoughts, the more honorable, upright, and effective we are; the greater our success; and the more blessed and enduring our achievements must be.

We can only rise, conquer, and achieve by lifting our thoughts.

We can only remain weak and abject and miserable by refusing to lift our thoughts.

There can be no progress, no achievement, without letting go of something. Our worldly success is proportionate to the release of our confused or indulgent thoughts and their replacement with directed focus on the development of our plans and the strengthening of our resolution and self-reliance.

> *Those who would accomplish little must sacrifice little.*
> *Those who would achieve much must sacrifice much.*
> *Those who would attain highly must sacrifice greatly.*

The Power of Directed Thought

All achievements, whether in the business, intellectual, or spiritual world, are the result of such definitely directed thought. They're governed by the same law and are of the same method. The only difference lies in the object of attainment.

Intellectual achievements are the result of thought devoted to the search for knowledge or for the beautiful and true in life and nature. Such achievements may be connected with vanity and ambition at times, but they're not the outcome of those characteristics. They are the natural outgrowth of long and arduous effort and of loving and unselfish thoughts.

Spiritual achievements are the realization of holy aspirations. Those who live constantly with noble and lofty thoughts and dwell on all that is loving and unselfish will become wise and noble in character. They will rise into positions of influence and blessedness just as surely as the sun reaches its zenith and the moon becomes full.

Achievement of whatever kind is the crown of endeavor, the diadem of thought. With self-control, resolution, clarity, righteousness, and well-directed thought we ascend. Through self-indulgence, slothfulness, toxicity, corruption, and confusion of thought we descend. We may rise to high success in the world and even to lofty altitudes in the spiritual realm, but we fall into weakness and wretchedness by allowing arrogant, selfish, and corrupt thoughts to run our lives. Victories attained by noble thought can only be maintained by watchfulness. Too many give way when success is assured and then rapidly fall back into failure.

So thought fearlessly joined with purpose becomes a creative force, and those who know this are ready to become something higher and stronger than those whose wavering thoughts and fluctuating sensations make them marks for any passing fad or advertisement. They become the conscious and intelligent wielders of their mental powers, achieving whatever they set their minds to accomplish.

Essential Points

- All that we achieve and all that we fail to achieve is the direct result of our own thoughts.
- Purpose, energy, the power to act and create, and all strong thoughts cease when doubt and fear creep in.
- Those who have conquered doubt and fear have conquered failure. Their every thought is allied with power, and all difficulties are bravely met and wisely overcome.
- Those whose first thought is indulgent can neither think clearly nor plan methodically.
- All achievements, whether in the business, intellectual, or spiritual world, are the result of definitely directed thought.

6

VISIONS AND IDEALS

Dreamers are the saviors of the world. As the visible world is sustained by the invisible, so humanity, through all of its many trials and tribulations, is nourished by the beautiful visions of its solitary dreamers. Humanity cannot forget them. It cannot let their ideals fade and die. It lives in them. It knows them in the realities it shall one day see and know.

Composer, sculptor, painter, poet, prophet, sage—these are the makers of the world, the architects of heaven. The world is beautiful because they have lived; without them, laboring humanity would perish. Columbus cherished a vision of another world, and he discovered it. Copernicus fostered the vision of a multiplicity of worlds and a wider universe, and he revealed it. The Buddha beheld the vision of a spiritual world of stainless beauty and perfect peace, and he entered into it.

Cherish your visions. Cherish your ideals. Cherish the music that stirs in your heart, the beauty that forms in your mind, the loveliness that drapes your finest thoughts, for out of them will grow all delightful conditions and heavenly environments, if you remain true to them. The greatest achievement was at first and for a time a dream. The oak sleeps in the acorn, the bird waits in the egg, and a waking angel stirs in the highest vision of the soul. Dreams are the seedlings of realities.

Those who cherish beautiful visions and lofty ideals in their hearts must one day realize them, for to desire is to obtain; to aspire is to achieve. Does it seem possible that our meanest desires would always be gratified, while our purest aspirations starve for lack of sustenance? Ask and you shall receive—whatever you want. Dream lofty dreams, and as you dream, so shall you become. Your vision is the promise of what you shall one day be. Your ideal is the prophecy of what you shall at last unveil.

Your circumstances may be uncomfortable now, for whatever reason, but they won't be for long if you simply perceive an ideal and strive to reach it. You cannot travel within and stand still without.

Applying the Laws of Thought

Consider a young woman hard-pressed by poverty and forced to work as a cheap laborer. She is unschooled, confined for long hours in an unhealthy sweatshop, and lacking all the arts of refinement. But she dreams of better things. She thinks of intelligence, of refinement, of grace and beauty. She conceives of, and mentally builds up, images of an ideal life. The vision of the wider liberty and a larger scope takes possession of her; unrest urges her to action. She utilizes all her spare time and means, small though they are, to develop her latent powers and resources.

Very soon her mind has become so altered that the sweatshop can no longer hold her. It's become so far out of harmony with her mental state that it falls out of her life as a garment is cast aside, and with more and more opportunities that fit the scope of her expanding powers, she passes out of it forever. It's a classic story, told in hundreds of novels and films, because it's true.

Years later we see this girl as a full-grown woman. We find her to be a ruler of the mind she wields with worldwide influence and almost unequaled power. In her hands, she holds the cords of gigantic responsibilities. She speaks, and, lo and behold, lives are changed. Men and women hang upon her words and remold their characters according to them, and, sun-like, she becomes the fixed and luminous center around which innumerable destinies revolve. She has realized the vision of her youth. She has become one with her ideal.

And you, too, gentle reader, will realize the true vision (not the idle wish) of your heart, be it base or beautiful or a mixture of both, for you will always gravitate toward what you secretly love most. Into your hands will be placed the exact results of your own thoughts; you will receive what you mentally earn, no more, no less. Whatever your present environment may be, you will fall, remain, or rise with your thoughts, your vision, your ideal. You will become as small as your controlling desire and as great as your dominant aspiration.

In the beautiful words of Stanton Kirkham Davis,

> You may be keeping accounts, and presently you shall walk out of the door that for so long has seemed to you the barrier of your ideals, and shall find yourself before an audience—the pen still behind your ear, the ink stains on your fingers—and then and there shall pour out the torrent of your inspiration. You may be driving sheep, and you shall wander to the city— bucolic and openmouthed; shall wander under the intrepid guidance of the spirit into the studio of the master, and after a time he shall say, "I have nothing more to teach you." Now you have become the master, who did so recently dream of great things while driving sheep. You shall lay down the saw and the plane to take upon yourself the regeneration of the world.[1]

The thoughtless, the ignorant, and the lazy, seeing only the apparent effects of things and not the things themselves, talk of luck, of fortune, of chance. They see people grow rich and say, "Look how lucky they are!" When someone else gets a raise, they call it favoritism. And seeing a saintly character with wide influence, they remark, "What good fortune that one has had!"

They don't see the trials and failures and struggles these men and women have voluntarily gone through to gain their experience. They can't know the sacrifices made, the efforts put forth, or the faith exercised to overcome what often appeared to be insurmountable obstacles as they moved toward the realization of their heart's vision.

They do not know the darkness and the heartaches,
but only see the light and joy and call it "luck."

They do not see the long and arduous journey,
but only behold the pleasant goal and call it "good fortune."

They do not understand the process,
but only perceive the result and call it "chance."

In all human affairs there are endeavors and there are results, and the strength of the endeavor is the measure of the result. It's not chance. Gifts, powers, and material, intellectual, and spiritual possessions are the fruits of endeavor. They are thoughts completed, objects accomplished, visions realized.

The vision that you glorify in your mind, the ideal that you enthrone in your heart—this will build your life and this you will become.

Essential Points

- You will always gravitate toward what you secretly love most. Into your hands will be placed the exact results of your own thoughts; you will receive that which you mentally earn, no more, no less.
- The thoughtless, the ignorant, and the slothful, seeing only the apparent effects of things and not the things themselves, talk of luck, of fortune, and chance.
- Gifts, powers, and material, intellectual, and spiritual possessions are thoughts completed, objects accomplished, visions realized.

7

SERENITY

A calm mind is one of the beautiful jewels of wisdom. It's the result of diligent self-management. It indicates understanding and effective use of the laws and operations of thought.

We can become calm to the extent that we understand and see ourselves as beings evolving from thought, and then we will understand others to be the result of thought as well. When we understand and see clearly the action of cause and effect in our inner life, we cease to fuss and fume and worry and grieve and instead remain poised, steadfast, and serene.

Those who have found calm have learned how to govern themselves. They know how to adapt their outward presence around others, and the people around them rely on and revere this spiritual strength, feeling that they can learn how to find calm too. The more tranquil we become, the greater our success, influence, and power for good. A business owner or manager, for example, will find that prosperity increases as she or he develops a greater self-control and equanimity, for people always prefer to deal with someone they feel good about.

People who are strong and calm are loved and revered. They're like a shade-giving tree in a thirsty land or a sheltering rock in a violent storm.

Who doesn't love a tranquil heart and a balanced, sweet-tempered soul? It doesn't matter whether it rains or shines or what changes come to those possessing these blessings, for they're always sweet, serene, and calm.

This exquisite poise of character that we call serenity is the last lesson to be learned. It's the flowering of life, the fruit of the soul. It's as precious as wisdom, more desirable than gold. How insignificant mere money-seeking looks in comparison with a serene life—a life that dwells in the ocean of Truth, beneath the waves, beyond the reach of tempests, in the eternal calm!

How many people do we know who sour their lives and ruin all that is sweet and beautiful with their explosive tempers, who destroy their poise of character and make bad blood! They are the tragic heroes and heroines—often the villains—of novels and plays. And how few people we meet in life who are well-balanced, who have the exquisite poise characteristic of the finished character! They are the heroes and heroines our hearts long to become.

Sadly, too much of humanity surges with uncontrolled passion and ungoverned grief. It is blown about by anxiety and doubt. Only the wise, whose thoughts are controlled and clarified, make the winds and the storms of their souls obey—and so experience serenity.

But tempest-tossed souls, wherever you may be, under whatever conditions you may live, know this:

In the ocean of life, the isles of blessedness are smiling;
the sunny shore of your ideal awaits your coming.
Keep your hand firmly upon the helm of thought.
In the ship of your soul reclines the commanding Ruler,
waiting to be awakened.
Self-control is strength;
Noble thought is mastery;
Calmness is power.
Say unto your heart, "Peace, be still!"

Essential Points

- A calm mind is one of the beautiful jewels of wisdom. It's the result of diligent self-management.
- As we understand and see clearly the action of cause and effect in our inner life, we cease to fuss, fume, worry, and grieve and instead remain poised, steadfast, and serene.
- Only the wise, whose thoughts are controlled and clarified, make the winds and the storms of their souls obey—and so experience serenity.

EXERCISES

---

1. The Purpose-Driven Experience

A. To see how purpose-driven thought works, think of a legitimate purpose, one that will make a difference in your life or the world. It may take the form of a spiritual ideal or it may be a worldly objective. Whatever it is, steadily focus the forces of your thought on this objective. Hold it as a strong intention in your heart and set out to accomplish it.

B. If, because of current circumstances, you're not prepared to take on a great purpose, focus your thoughts on performing your current duty perfectly, no matter how insignificant the task may appear. Only in this way can the thoughts be gathered and focused and resolution and energy developed. This being done, there is nothing that cannot be accomplished.

C. Having defined your purpose, mentally mark out a straight path to its achievement. This is where you "plan your work and then work your plan," as the famous coach Vince Lombardi is credited with saying. If you want to write or draw your plan, it helps to start at the desired end and then write the final step that leads to that end, and then the step (or steps) that lead to that step, and so forth, all the way back to this place and time. Sometimes a big sheet of paper works better than a list, with the desired result on one end (or in the center) of the sheet and circles and arrows mapping the steps to it. Once you've made your plan, set it aside for use as a reference if you find yourself off track.

D. Now, for twenty-eight days, make this purpose the central point of your thoughts. Make it your number one priority and devote yourself to its attainment, not allowing your thoughts to wander away into fantasies, longings, doubts, or imaginings. Start each day imagining its fulfillment; then go through the day "working the plan." This doesn't mean you have to do exactly what your original chart says. It does mean always being open to the opportunities that natural law always provides. End each day writing or charting your progress, focusing on what *has* been accomplished rather than what hasn't.

This is the royal road to self-management and true concentration of thought. Even though you may fail again and again until all habits of weakness are overcome and you fully accomplish your purpose (as you necessarily must to be freed of those weaknesses), the inner strength gained is the measure of your true success. It will form a new starting point for future efforts, moving you into greater and greater power and triumph.

2. As Within, So Without

A. To experience the world and people around you changing as a result of changes in your inner state, make a list of the people you have the most trouble with in your world. Write next to each one the nature of the problem you have with them.

B. Now take a look at the problems you've had with these people and see if they cluster together. You may, for instance, feel as if some people have betrayed your trust or that others don't listen to you. On a separate page, list these clustered patterns and name the people who fit them below each one.

C. Start a new page for each pattern with the words "I am never upset for the reason I think" and then describe all the times you've experienced that pattern, going as far back as you can remember, to the very first time, if possible. See the connections between the various events and people, the decisions you made about the world and other people because of them, and the choices you made to help bring about the experiences later in life.

D. Now pick one pattern and imagine each of the people associated with that pattern sitting in front of you, one by one. Tell each of them, in your imagination, what you've learned and how their actions fit into a pattern in your life. Tell them how, when you think about it, the experience wasn't completely their fault. Ask them to forgive you for putting all the blame on them for something you helped bring about. Tell them you're ready to stop blaming them and are letting go of all the emotions you've stored up around this experience.

E. Now, as you're telling each one of them these things, imagine a powerful beam of light from above surrounding both of you, flooding and cleansing both of you, and dissolving any and all distress between you. Let it remain until all you feel when you imagine each of these people is the appreciation, or even love, you would feel for anyone who's played a significant role in your life—not a romantic feeling but a deep appreciation for who they've been and the history you share. Your body will relax when you feel this and a smile may form. At this point, get up and take a shower. Let the water flow over you and imagine it's flowing *through* you to help you bring this feeling into the physical world.

F. Now you can claim a new form of relationship between you and this pattern. You can say it in a sentence—something like, "I am freed of this pattern of _____ ," or "I am free to live my life in love and safety and to trust all I meet," or "I am loved and loving; everyone in my life is sharing that love with me in healthy and harmonious ways," or whatever powerfully states the way you'd like to be living from now on.

G. Allow yourself to imagine what your life now can be like. Feel what it's like to be free of this pattern, able to move through life without being afraid of it or avoiding it or getting upset over it. Feel the freedom and the joy. Appreciate that feeling.

H. Finally, put all your writing away. At least three weeks after you've completed the exercise, take a look at it and write down the changes you've seen in the people and in the pattern itself. (If any part of the pattern comes up again, do the exercise again. You'll free up the next layer of the "onion" of your personality, and it will get less intense and easier each time, until one day it's all gone.)

LIGHT ON LIFE

INTRODUCTION: THE LIGHT OF WISDOM

When you enter a dark room and can't see the things around you, it's not very easy to get around. If you make any sudden moves, you're liable to bump into something and hurt yourself. But when you turn on a light, all confusion disappears immediately; every object is visible and there's no danger of being hurt.

For many people, life is like a dark room, and their suffering is caused by bumping up against things—not objects but laws and principles—that they don't see and therefore aren't prepared to deal with. But when the light of wisdom shines into their darkened awareness, their confusion vanishes, difficulties dissolve, and all things are seen in their true place and proportion. Then they're able to walk open-eyed and unhurt in the clear light of understanding.[1]

1

THE SIMPLE FACTS OF LIFE

We live in an age defined by freedom of thought and expression, but with such freedoms come conflict and confusion. Never have there been so many religious sects, occult philosophies, and other schools of thought—and all are eager to sell us their explanation of the universe. The contradictions among them are so confusing and disturbing that it is almost impossible for anyone seeking Truth to find a rock-solid refuge.

With so much uncertainty around us, we're forced to turn and look within ourselves for the answers. And when we do, the simple, undeniable facts of our nature and our being stand out clearly against the controversy and confusion. Their eternal harmony attracts us; they appeal to us with their simplicity and truth. So we discover that the answers we seek are always within us. Indeed, they are our life.

To get to these simple facts of our nature and being, it's important to realize that conflict and confusion are based on hypotheses, not facts. Facts are fixed and final, and they contain within themselves the groundwork of all knowledge concerning them; hypotheses are variable and vanishing. The clear perception of one fact will lead to other facts, but the assumption that leads to a hypothesis, while appearing to throw light upon a fact, in reality covers it up.

In this day and age, many people aren't even aware of the beautiful simplicity and inherent power of facts. They don't see the intrinsic loveliness of Truth but must always add to it. So when a fact is named, the question that usually comes up is, "How can we explain it?" This question is then followed by a hypothesis, which leads to another hypothesis, and so on, until the fact is completely lost in the mass of contradictory explanations. This is how so much controversy and confusion arises.

We can't experience the splendor of Truth while playing with the gaudy toys of pretty hypotheses. Truth is not an opinion, nor can any opinion enlarge or adorn it. Fact and conjecture are eternally separate, and while clever intellectual jugglery may entertain and deceive even the greatest of minds, it cannot in the slightest degree alter a fact or affect the nature of things as they are.

Because of this, true teachers abandon the devious path of explanation and deal only with the simple facts of life, fixing the students' attention upon these, instead of increasing confusion by adding their own explanations to an already bewildering maze of conjecture.

We don't need to go beyond our own being to find wisdom. These facts of life, which are ever before us, can be understood and known every moment if we just abandon the blinding delusions that egotism creates. We are all living, thinking beings; *as we think, so we are*. The perception and realization of these facts alone—of being and thinking—lead us toward the highest wisdom and perfection.

Essential Points

- For many people, life is like a dark room, and their suffering is caused by sudden contact with principles that they don't see and therefore aren't prepared to deal with. But in the clear light of understanding, they're able to walk open-eyed and unhurt.
- The answers we seek are always within us; indeed, they are our life.
- Facts are fixed and final, and they contain within themselves the groundwork of all knowledge concerning them.
- We don't need to go beyond our own being to find wisdom; as we think, so we are.

2

AS YOU THINK

One of the reasons some religious people don't walk in the light of wisdom is that they fill their days with speculation about a soul they believe to be separate from their mind. But this idea of a separate soul blinds them to their actual nature and being. They look outside themselves for their source and so are unable to know themselves. As a result, they're unaware of the nature of their own thoughts, which literally means they have no conscious life.

To occupy ourselves with the investigation of things separate from mind and thought is pure speculation. Mind, thought, and life are as inseparable as light, radiance, and color. None of us can be separated from our mind; our life cannot be separated from our thoughts.

What's more, by the universal law of evolution, the mind is not something "ready-made" but subject to change, and it has within it a great capacity for progress. Our being is modified by every thought we think. Every experience affects our character. Every effort we make changes our mentality. We're not only the product of our thoughts but also constantly becoming what we will be.

Seeing that we're the product of our thoughts and that these thoughts are subject to change, it logically follows that to deliberately change our thoughts is to change ourselves. Here lies the secret of our downfall—but also of our power and freedom—for to live is to think and act, and to think and act is to change. Even if people are ignorant of the nature of their thoughts, they will continue to change, for better and worse. However, once we understand the nature of thought, the process of change can be sped up and directed for the better. We just need to apply this law of change by focusing our thought on the highest principle we can conceive, to experience the peace, freedom, and joy that is our goal.

All religions embody this universal law of change, working on the hearts and minds of people to direct them into purer and higher channels. Partial or complete success in this direction, which some call salvation, is simply the shift from one kind of thought—one condition of mind—into a more enlightened state of mind.

It's true that most religionists today don't know this fact; the veil of hypotheses gets between them and their awareness. But the great teachers who founded the various spiritual traditions built their teachings on this fact. Their essential precepts—purifying the heart, thinking right thoughts, and doing good deeds—prove the point. These and the other principles that those teachers stressed and reiterated are simply calls to a higher and nobler mode of thought, urging us to choose those thoughts that lift us into the realms of greater power, greater good, and greater bliss.

Each of us can save ourselves from ourselves—from our own folly and suffering—by creating new habits of thought, by becoming a new thinker, by evolving into a new person. And aspiration, meditation, and devotion are the primary means that people in all ages have employed to reach higher modes of thought, more profound levels of peace, and vaster realms of knowledge, for *as we think, so we are.*

The Theravada Buddhist sutras include the story of a man, neither very wise nor pious, who asks the Buddha how to attain the highest wisdom and enlightenment. The Buddha replies, "By ceasing all craving."[1] It's recorded that the man let go of all personal cravings and at once realized the highest wisdom and enlightenment. There's also a saying in Buddhism that "the only miracle with which the wise concern themselves is the transformation of sinner into a saint."

As an example from the Christian tradition, if anyone were, by a supreme effort, to succeed in having "that mind which was in Christ" (Philippians 2:5), which means thinking as Jesus thought—not by imitation but by a sudden realization of indwelling power—that person would be unified with Jesus as Christ.

Emerson referred to this transforming power of change of thought when he said, "It is as easy to be great as to be small," which is very like the biblical saying "Be ye therefore perfect, even as your Father which is in Heaven is perfect."[2]

And, after all, what is the fundamental difference between a great person and a lesser one? It must be thought, mental attitude. True, it's also knowledge, but then knowledge can't be separated from thought. Throughout the whole range of human life, thought determines character, condition, and knowledge, and every substitution of a better thought for a worse one marks an important transformation of mind and advance in knowledge.

Essential Points

- None of us can be separated from our mind; our life cannot be separated from our thoughts.
- We are the sum total of our thoughts, and since these thoughts are subject to change, it follows that to deliberately change our thoughts is to change ourselves.
- Aspiration, meditation, and devotion are the primary means that people in all ages have employed to reach higher modes of thought, more profound levels of peace, and vaster realms of knowledge.
- Every substitution of a better thought for a worse one marks an important transformation of mind and advance in knowledge.

3

REPLACING SLAVE MENTALITY
WITH SAGE MENTALITY

The mass of humanity, unenlightened about our spiritual nature, moves slowly along the evolutionary path. It's urged on by the blind impulse of the culture's dominant thoughts and is stimulated and influenced by external things. But the true thinker, the sage, travels swiftly and intelligently along a chosen path of his or her own.

We can say, then, that the multitudes are the slaves of thought, but the sage is its ruler. The slave follows blindly, while the sage chooses intelligently. Slaves obey the impulse of the moment, thinking of their immediate pleasure and happiness; the sage commands and subdues impulse, resting in permanence. Slaves, following blind impulse, violate the laws of righteousness; the sage, not distracted by impulse, obeys the law of righteousness. The sage stands face-to-face with the facts of life, knowing the nature of thought, understanding and heeding the law of his or her being.

The sage—intelligent, radiant, calm—and the fool—confused, darkened, disturbed—are one in essence, divided only by the nature of their thoughts. But even the sorrow-burdened victim of blind impulse can open the mind's eye to see the true nature of things when he or she wishes to, so when the fool abandons foolish thoughts and chooses wise thoughts, lo and behold, the slave becomes a sage.

Just as Socrates saw the essential oneness of virtue and knowledge, so does every sage. But while the pursuit of knowledge may aid and accompany wisdom, it does not itself lead to wisdom. In other words, someone may have plenty of "book smarts" but be foolish in the school of life. Only choosing wise thoughts and noble thinking results in wise and noble deeds. Such a choice then leads to revelations of true knowledge and the attainment of wisdom.

Folly and wisdom, ignorance and enlightenment are not merely the result of thought; they are thought itself. Both cause and effect are contained in thought. If we hold to this truth, it follows that

If you're lost in controversy and confusion, you can find yourself.

You can see yourself as you are.
You are the thinker and doer, the actor and knower.
You are desire and sorrow, joy and suffering, love and hate.
All of these, as one composite mentality, make up the being that is you.

Thus, you are not a being that possesses a soul.
Nor is your mind an instrument of a metaphysical, superhuman soul.
Your spiritual nature is rounded by your sphere of thought.

You are soul.
Your mind is being.

You are mind.

When we're prepared to turn from the illusory and self-created world of hypotheses where we often wander and instead stand face-to-face with the actuality of our being, then each of us will walk in the clear light of wisdom and know ourselves as we are. And in that place we can do more. We can picture ourselves as we would wish to be and create within us the new thinker, the new self.

Now is the time to choose, for every moment in life is the time of choice—and every hour is destiny.

All that we are is the result of what we have thought.
It is founded on our thoughts; it is made up of our thoughts.

Essential Points

- The multitudes are the slaves of thought, but the sage is its ruler. The slave follows blindly, while the sage chooses intelligently.
- When we're prepared to turn from the illusory and self-created world of hypotheses and instead stand face-to-face with the actuality of our being, then each of us will walk in the clear light of wisdom and know ourselves as we are—free.
- Now is the time to choose.

EXERCISES

A. Set aside a few hours in a comfortable place with the means to write. Sit quietly for a while and remember the times in your life and the people you've known or heard about that bring happy, joyous feelings as you think of them. Then make a list of whoever or whenever comes to mind.

B. Consider those times and those people and write down some of their qualities. If the time was a family holiday, words like *comfort, love, joking,* and *beauty* may come to mind. If it was when you accomplished something, you may think of words like *satisfaction, fulfillment,* and *pride.* If the person was someone you know, words like *loving, fun, helpful,* and *wise* might come to mind. If you think of people you've only heard about, write down what about them leads you to feel good when you think of them.

C. Now take this list of times and people, with their qualities, and consider your own possible future. Consider the following: What would your life look like if it always included all those qualities? What would you be doing? Where would you be living? Whom would you be working with, playing with, loving?

D. Write down some of the ideas that come to mind. You may want to write them into a story, in a letter to someone from your future self, or simply as a list of activities, thoughts, feelings, and people.

E. Read what you've written and imagine living that life. Feel what it's like to live that way.

F. Modify what you've written as necessary to keep the feelings happy, peaceful, joyful, and loving.

G. Once you're satisfied with your description, put it in a place where you can read it every day for twenty-eight days. Make a commitment that you'll look at it and feel it in as much detail as you can, with as many inner senses as possible (seeing colors, feeling textures, hearing sounds, and so forth) at least once every day.

H. Now go about your normal life and watch the changes—and don't be surprised if many of the things you've been doing or are used to having or seeing fall away to make room for the new you!

TO RISE ABOVE

INTRODUCTION: ABOVE THE WORLD

We can't avoid the turmoil of the world, nor can we alter external objects, shape other people to our liking, or mold the cosmos to our wishes. However, we can change internal things—our desires, passions, thoughts—to bring our wishes and expectations into harmony with the natural laws in the world around us. In doing so, we rise above anxiety over the duties and difficulties of life that constantly try to claim our attention. This opens the door to more harmonious experiences.

> *Surrounded by noise, we can have a quiet mind.*
> *Involved in responsibilities, the heart can be at rest.*
> *In the midst of strife, we can know an abiding peace.*

The twenty essays in this section of the book, unrelated as some of them seem to be, are in fact harmonious in spirit. Together, they point to heights of self-knowledge and self-conquest that lift the reader above the turbulence of the world into a space where heavenly peace reigns.

1

TRUE HAPPINESS

We're deluding ourselves if we imagine that we can make the world happier by spreading any theory or theology without first lifting ourselves above malice, fear, and unhappiness. To maintain a pleasant attitude, to think only thoughts that are loving and gentle, to be happy under all circumstances, this must be the aim of all those who wish to lessen the misery of the world. It's the essence of Mohandas K. Gandhi's famous statement that "we must be the change we wish to see in the world."

Those who are unpleasant or unloving or who promote unhappiness in the people around them are adding to the world's misery. But those who continually live in goodwill and happiness are increasing the world's happiness day by day—all this being independent of any religious or social beliefs they may or may not hold. Those who've not yet learned how to be gentle, giving, loving, and happy have really acquired very little knowledge, however great their book-learning or profound their worldly experience. For it's in the process of becoming gentle, loving, and happy that the deep, real, and enduring lessons of life are learned.

Unbroken grace in the face of all hostility or challenge is the unfailing mark of a soul that has witnessed wisdom, conquered the lesser self, and now possesses Truth. Such a sweet and happy soul is the ripened fruit of experience and wisdom, casting an invisible yet powerful influence around them, gladdening the hearts of others and purifying the world.

All those who strive for happiness but have not yet begun to live with the dignity of a true and noble life need not be distressed; they may begin today if they so choose. Now is always the moment of choice.

But don't say that your surroundings are against you. Your surroundings are never against you; they are there to aid you. All the turbulence and turmoil of the outside world over that cause us to lose our pleasant and peaceful state of mind are the very conditions necessary to our development, and it's only by meeting and overcoming them that we can learn and grow and ripen. If there's any fault, it's in us, not external things.

Pure happiness is the ·rightful and healthy condition of the soul, and all may possess it if they will live choosing the highest, most ideal option in all situations.

> *Have goodwill*
> *To all that lives, letting unkindness die,*
> *And greed and wrath, so that your lives be made*
> *Like soft airs passing by.*[1]

If this seems too difficult for you, then unrest and unhappiness will continue to be your experience. But fear not; your belief, your desire, and your resolve are all that's needed to make the shift to a blessed inner state.

Gloom and doom, anxiety and irritability, condemnation and grumbling—all these are thought-cancers, mind-diseases. They're indications of a mental condition that serves no one, and those who suffer from them would do well to shift their thinking and conduct.

It's true that there is misery in the world, so much that all our love and compassion are needed. But our misery will not help the situation;

there's too much of that in the world already. No, it is our cheerfulness and happiness that are needed, for there's far too little of that.

We can give nothing better to the world than beauty of life and character. Without this, all other actions are vain. This truth is enduring, real, and not to be overthrown; it includes all joy and blessedness. If you would have others be true, then be true yourself. If you would have the world emancipated from all misery and suffering, then emancipate yourself. If you want your home and your surroundings to be happy, then be happy. You can transform everything around you if you simply transform yourself.

> *Cease to dwell pessimistically upon the wrongs around you.*
> *Revolt against seeing evil in others and forgive them their trespasses.*
> *Commence to live free from all wrongdoing and*
> *fearful thought yourself.*

Peace of mind, pure spirituality, and real social transformation lie this way.

> *Don't bewail and bemoan . . .*
> *Don't waste yourself in rejection, nor bark against the bad,*
> *But chant the beauty of the good.*[2]

And this you will naturally and spontaneously do as you realize the good in yourself.

Essential Points

- We're deluding ourselves if we imagine that we can make the world happier without lifting ourselves above malice, fear, and unhappiness.
- Those who have not yet learned how to be gentle, giving, loving, and happy have really acquired very little knowledge, however great their book-learning or profound their worldly experience.
- Don't say that your surroundings are against you. Your surroundings are never against you; they're there to aid you.

- If there's any fault, it's in us, not external things.
- Your belief, your desire, and your resolve are all that's needed to make the shift to a blessed inner state.
- You can transform everything around you if you simply transform yourself.

2

BECOMING IMMORTAL

I mmortality is not a speculative something beyond the grave; it's here and now. It's a lucid state of consciousness in which the sensations of the body, the varying states of mind, and the circumstances and events of life are seen as fleeting and understood to be illusions.

Immortality does not belong to time and will never be found in time; it belongs to eternity. And just as time is here and now, so eternity is here and now.

To find eternity and establish ourselves in it, we must overcome the self that derives its life from the unsatisfying and perishable things in time. As long as we remain immersed in the sensations, desires, and passing events of a day-to-day existence and regard them as the essential components of life, we can have no knowledge of immortality.

What most people desire, which they often mistake for immortality, is the continuous succession of sensations and events in time. But people who love and cling to the things that stimulate and supply their immediate gratification, realizing no state of consciousness above and beyond it, only thirst for the continuance of this basic existence. They're trying to banish the thought that they will eventually have to part from the earthly luxuries and delights they've become enslaved to and that they think are somehow a part of themselves.

This persistence of sequence is the antithesis of immortality, and to be absorbed in it is spiritual death. Life's very nature is change, impermanence. It is a continual living and dying.

In spite of the teachings of the spiritualists, the death of the body can never lead to immortality. Disincarnate spirits can't be different from us; they live little feverish lives of broken consciousness, still immersed in change and mortality. Those mortals who thirst for the persistence of their pleasure-loving personality are still mortal after death and only live another life with a beginning and an end—a life without memory of the past or knowledge of the future. They're what the Buddha called "hungry ghosts," and they're the reason that biblical prophets warned against going to mediums for understanding, rather than turning inside to the higher wisdom of the divine within. While there may be wise beings who are no longer in their bodies, simply having passed on from this life is not a guarantee of wisdom.

Life consists of an ever-moving procession of events, and in this procession, mortals are immersed and carried along with it—and being so carried along, they have no knowledge of what is behind or before them. Immortals, on the other hand, are those who have detached themselves from the limitations of time by having ascended into a state of consciousness that is fixed and invariable. They're not affected by passing events and sensations but have stepped out of this procession, standing by, unmoving, while watching it. And from their fixed place, they see the before, the behind, and the middle of the moving procession of events called life. No longer identifying themselves with the sensations and fluctuations of the personality, or with the external changes that make up a life in time, they've become the passionless spectators of their own destinies and of the destiny of the world.

Mortals live their lives in a state of consciousness that has an earthbound sense of time that begins and ends. Immortals are those who live in the cosmic state of consciousness, in which there is neither beginning nor end but an eternal now. Immortals remain poised and steadfast under all changes, and the death of their bodies does not in any way interrupt the eternal consciousness they abide in; they've simply cast off a garment.

Mortals are like those caught in a dream—they neither know that they were formerly awake nor that they will wake again. They are dreamers without knowledge, nothing more. Immortals, however, are those who have awakened from their dreams and know that their dreaming was not an enduring reality but a passing illusion. They are those with true wisdom, the knowledge of both states—that of persistence and that of immortality—and they are in full possession of themselves.

In the Christian tradition, it is said of a believer that "he shall not taste of death" because Jesus stepped out of the stream of mortality and established himself in the abode of Truth so that all humanity could see and know the possibility. Bodies, personalities, nations, and worlds pass away but Truth remains, and its glory is undimmed by time.

The immortals, then, are those who have conquered themselves. They no longer identify themselves with the self-seeking forces of the personality but have trained themselves to direct these forces with the hand of a master. They have thus brought themselves into harmony with the causal energy and source of all things. When we focus our hearts and minds on the eternal and unchangeable verities, the fretful worry of life ceases, doubt and fear are cast out, and death becomes nothing for those who have realized the fadeless splendor of a life of Truth.

Essential Points

- Immortality is not a speculative something beyond the grave; it's here and now.
- What most people desire, which they mistake for immortality, is the continuous succession of sensations and events in time.
- Immortals have detached themselves from the things of time by having ascended into a state of consciousness that is not affected by passing events and sensations.

- No longer identifying themselves with the sensations and fluctuations of the personality, or with the external changes that make up a life in time, they've become the passionless spectators of their own destinies and of the destiny of the world.
- The immortals, then, are those who have conquered themselves. They have brought themselves into harmony with the causal energy and source of all things.

3

OVERCOMING SELF

M any people have confused and misinformed notions about what
"overcoming self," "eradication of desire," and "annihilation of
the personality" mean. These concepts are fundamental to the inner
teachings of virtually all spiritual traditions, from the Buddhist idea of
nonattachment to the Christian idea of dying to the self and being
born again to the shamanic little death experience. Nonetheless, confusion continues. Some think it's all metaphysical theory, totally unrelated
to normal life and action, while others conclude that it's the crushing
out of all life, energy, and action—almost stagnation and death. These
misunderstandings can be corrected only by the individuals themselves,
but it may be a little easier if the concept is presented in another way.

The doctrine of overcoming or annihilating the self is simplicity
itself. In fact, it's so simple, practical, and close at hand that a five-year-
old, whose mind is not yet clouded with theories, theological schemes,
and speculative philosophies, can understand it more easily than many
adults. They've not yet lost the simple and beautiful truths and replaced
them with complicated theories.

The annihilation of self consists merely in weeding out and
destroying all those thoughts, beliefs, memories, and assumptions that
lead to division, strife, suffering, disease, and sorrow—the characteristics

of our small, egoic self. It does not mean the destruction of the good, beautiful, and peace-producing qualities of our true nature, which in Sanskrit is called Atman, and which Ralph Waldo Emerson calls the Self, Wayne Dyer calls our Sacred Self, and Emilie Cady calls our Individuality.[1] For instance, when we're tempted to irritability or anger, and by a great effort overcome this selfish tendency, cast it from us, and act instead from our inner essence that is patience and love, in that moment we practice the annihilation of self.

Every noble person is called so because they practice this. They're like noble metals that have been freed from any impurities, glowing with the heat of wisdom, unaffected by the conditions of their environments. And those who carry out this practice to its completion have eradicated every selfish tendency until only the divinely beautiful qualities remain. They've annihilated all the elements of the small self, the ego. We call them noble; they have arrived at Truth.

In the Buddhist tradition, the Noble Path is one of nonattachment and right choices. By releasing the small self's attachments to objects and ways of thinking or doing things and then consistently choosing rightly (right livelihood, right relationship, and so on), the follower of the Path gently leaves behind the old tendencies and embodies the noble being that's called the Buddha Nature.

In the Christian tradition, the image of Jesus's body crucified is the metaphor for overcoming the small self and allowing the Christ Self to lift the believer above circumstances and become immortal. The apostle Paul instructs us to "let that mind that was in Christ Jesus be in you" (Philippians 2:5).

The self to be annihilated is the small, egoic self, sometimes called the ego or lesser self, which Emilie Cady calls the personality.[2] It emerges out of the fear of separation from our Source and develops in the course of our lives to maintain that separation. It has the following ten worthless and sorrow-producing characteristics:

1. Lust
2. Hostility

3. Greed
4. Self-indulgence
5. Self-seeking
6. Vanity
7. Pride
8. Doubt
9. Beliefs and assumptions based on fear
10. Delusion

Overcoming the small self, the personality, is accomplished in the total abandonment and complete annihilation of these ten elements. In the Buddhist tradition, these are the qualities that lead to all forms of suffering, and the purpose of meditation is to discover and move past each of them. In the Christian tradition they are the Seven Deadly Sins expanded a little, and the disciplines of the monastic traditions are designed to help replace them with the Seven Virtues. In his auto-biography, Benjamin Franklin describes how, as he was returning from several wild years in England as a young man, he determined to eradi-cate these vices from his mind and actions and replace them with their opposites.

In a wonderful way, the practice of eradicating these undesirable elements also teaches the cultivation, experience, and preservation of the following ten divine qualities:

1. Clear, undistracted focus
2. Patience
3. Humility
4. Surrender
5. Self-reliance
6. Fearlessness
7. Knowledge
8. Wisdom
9. Compassion
10. Love

These compose the Body of Truth, and to live entirely in them is to be a doer and knower of the Truth, an embodiment of Truth. The combination of the first ten elements makes up the small self, or the personality; the combination of the ten qualities resulting from this practice produces what is called Truth, the impersonal, the abiding, real, immortal—our true, Sacred Self, or Individuality.

Clearly, then, overcoming self is not depriving us of gladness, happiness, and joy. Instead, it's constantly experiencing these delights and living with these joy-filling qualities; it's abandoning the lust for enjoyment but not enjoyment itself; it's the destruction of the thirst for pleasure but not pleasure itself. It's also the annihilation of selfish longings for love, power, and possessions and the preservation of all those things that draw us together in unity and harmony.

Far from the idealization of stagnation and death, the practice of annihilation of the small self's tendencies urges us to develop the qualities that lead to our highest, most effective, and enduring action and life. Those whose actions proceed from some or all of the ten earthbound sorrow-producing elements waste their energy on negatives and keep their souls in bondage. But those whose actions proceed from the ten qualities of Truth act truly and wisely and so free their souls.

People who live largely in the ten earthbound elements of the personality or small self are blind and deaf to the higher spiritual truths and will find no attraction in the doctrine of self-surrender, for it looks to them like the complete extinction of their beings. However, those who strive to live in the ten heavenly qualities will see their glory and beauty and will know this practice as the foundation of eternal life. They will also see that when they understand and practice it, every worldly activity will be intensified and enlarged, while freed from strife and pain.

Essential Points

- The annihilation of self consists merely in weeding out and destroying all those thoughts, beliefs, memories, and assumptions that lead to division, strife, suffering, disease, and sorrow.

- Overcoming of self is not depriving us of gladness, happiness, and joy, but rather the constant possession of these things and living with these joy-filling qualities.
- Those whose actions proceed from some or all of the ten earthbound sorrow-producing elements waste their energy on negatives.
- Those whose actions proceed from the ten qualities of Truth act truly and wisely and so free their souls.

4

THE USES OF TEMPTATION

The human soul, in its journey toward perfection, passes through three distinct stages.

The first is the animal stage, in which people are content to live in the gratification of their senses, unaware of their divine inheritance, and altogether unconscious of the spiritual possibilities within.

The second is the dual stage. This is when temptation plays its part in the progress of the soul, for in this stage the mind is constantly oscillating between its animal and divine tendencies, having awakened to the awareness of both. It's a stage of falling and rising, gaining and losing. The soul is reluctant to leave behind the gratifications it has lived with for so long, yet aspires to the clarity and power of the spiritual state. No wonder people in this stage are continually frustrated by an undecided choice! This is when the personality—the egoic, small self—takes form.

Urged on, however, by the divine life within it—whatever anguish and suffering were experienced in the second stage—the soul is ushered into the third stage, that of knowledge, in which it rises above both fear and temptation, and enters into peace.

Temptation, like fear, is not the lasting condition that most people believe it is. It's a passing phase—an experience that the soul must pass through. But whether people pass through this condition in their present lives—and realize holiness and a heavenly world in the here and now—or not, depends entirely upon the strength of their intellectual and spiritual efforts and on the intensity and earnestness of their search for Truth.

Temptation, with all its dark torments, can be overcome here and now. But finding oneself in the dark can only be remedied by turning on the light of wisdom and fully understanding the source, nature, and meaning of temptation. Only then can it finally be dissolved and our souls rest from their long travail. For the fully enlightened soul is proof against all temptation; as long as ignorance remains, no amount of praying, candle lighting, or other kinds of spiritual observances will bring peace.

It's commonly known that those who wage war on their enemies but know nothing of their foes' strengths, weaknesses, or tactics will fail miserably in battle and fall speedily into enemy hands. Sadly, many people who wish to overcome temptation make the same mistake. They make temptation their sworn enemy without knowing their foe. They search outside themselves for temptation's stronghold, its place of hiding. They guard the gates of their minds as if it were a fortress, lest temptation make a stealthy entrance without them seeing.

This battle against temptation is the holy warfare of the saints—and the fight every soul joins when it awakens out of its long sleep of animal indulgence. But many people fail to overcome temptation, and the fight is indefinitely prolonged, because they believe, almost universally, the delusion that all temptations come from outside us.

Still, Truth must always show itself, so their continual worry, ceaseless watchfulness, and constant and rigid introspection ultimately leads them to discover the vain and selfish motives of their own souls. They begin to see that the source and cause of all temptation is in their own inner craving. Then, when this is purified or eliminated, external objects and activities become utterly powerless to move them toward temptation.

And so one truth must be realized about this delusion: temptation comes from within. The idea that God, a devil, evil spirits, or any people or objects are the source of temptation must be dispelled. We're tempted because certain ideas within us lead us toward temptation. These ideas may lie dormant for a long time, and we may think we've gotten rid of them, when suddenly, in the presence of a person or object, the craving wakes up and demands immediate gratification. This is the mental state we call temptation.

Clearly the outer object is merely the occasion of the temptation, never the cause. The craving is within the one tempted; if the cause were in the object, we all would be tempted alike, temptation could never be overcome, and we would be hopelessly doomed to endless torment.

As long as this delusion holds us in bondage, we make no progress. But when we shake this shackle away, we move quickly from victory to victory, experiencing spiritual joy and rest. This is what Jesus and the Buddha were trying to tell us and what *A Course in Miracles* is designed to help us experience.[1]

The essential goodness in us, our Individuality, is never tempted. Goodness dissolves temptation. Those who are honest can't be tempted to steal, even if it were easy to do so. Those with purified appetites cannot be tempted to gluttony and drunkenness, though the platter of food and wine might be most luscious. Those who hold an enlightened understanding, whose minds are calm in the strength of their clarity, can never be tempted to anger, irritability, or revenge. The wiles and charms of the wanton fall upon the purified heart as empty, meaningless shadows.

If you are tempted, then, know that you tempted yourself. "For everyone is tempted when drawn away of their own lust and enticed," said the apostle James (James 1:14).

The degree of temptations we experience is directly related to our own lack of clarity: the thoughts, beliefs, and assumptions we hold that are based in fear, lack, and the idea of separation from our Source. This means we have the remedy in our own hands; we can become victorious over all temptation by releasing those ideas from our hearts and minds, for as we purify our heart, temptation ceases. When an idea has been released from the heart, the object that formerly appealed to it can no longer do so but instead lies there, powerless, with nothing left in us that responds to it.

Temptation, therefore, is best understood as a way to urge us on to higher levels of knowledge and clarity. Without temptation, the soul cannot grow and become strong and move beyond the dual stage and into its true power. There could be no wisdom, no real virtue, and though there would still be apathy and death, there could be no peace or fullness of life without the experience of temptation. When temptation is understood and overcome, perfection is assured. So let's search diligently for the ideas we hold that no longer serve us, realizing that while we're subject to temptation, we have much to learn and understand through it.

Temptation entices us because the small, egoic self is unwilling to let go. It's a false, mortal self, devoid of all true knowledge, acting only on its own immediate gratification, ignorant of every Truth and every divine principle. If you cling to that lesser self, you will continually suffer the pains of three separate torments: the torment of desire, the torment of repletion, and the torment of remorse.

> *So flame of Trishna,[2] lust and thirst of things.*
> *Eager, ye cleave to shadows, dote on dreams;*
> *A false self in the midst ye plant, and make*
> *A world around which seems*
> *Blind to the height beyond; deaf to the sound*
> *Of sweet airs breathed from far past Indra's sky;[3]*
> *Dumb to the summons of the true life kept*
> *For him who false puts by,*
> *So grow the strife and lust which make earth's war,*
> *So grieve poor cheated hearts and flow salt tears;*
> *So wax the passions, envies, angers, hates;*
> *So years chase blood-stained years*
> *With wild red feet.[4]*

In that small, egoic self lies the germ of every suffering, the blight of every hope, the substance of every grief. When you're ready to give it up—when you're willing to have it laid bare before you in all its selfishness, toxicity, and ignorance, and to release its darkness completely—then you will begin to experience the joys of a life of self-knowledge and self-mastery. You'll become conscious of your own divine nature, which, seeking no gratification, abides in a state of perpetual joy and peace where suffering cannot come and temptation can find no foothold. Establishing yourself, day by day, more and more firmly in that inner divinity, the time will at last come when temptation is powerless against you.

Essential Points

- Temptation, like fear, is not a lasting condition as most people believe it is. It's a passing phase—an experience the soul must pass through.

- Many people who wish to overcome temptation search outside themselves, but the outer object is merely the occasion of the temptation, never the cause. The craving is within the one tempted.

- The thoughts, beliefs, and assumptions we hold that are based in fear, lack, and the idea of separation from our Source are the cause of all temptation, and we can overcome it by releasing and replacing those ideas.

- Temptation is a means of urging us on to higher levels of knowledge and clarity. Without temptation, the soul can't grow and become strong and move beyond the dual level to our full power.

5

THE SOUL OF INTEGRITY

There are times in the lives of everyone who has chosen to live from the ten divine qualities described in chapter 3, "Overcoming Self," when their faith in and knowledge of those principles is tested to the utmost. The way these fiery trials end decides whether we have sufficient strength to live in Truth and join the company of the free or remain a slave and a hireling to the cruelest taskmaster: our own small, ego self. After all, it's not the lash of the whip or the chains that make a slave but the mind of the enslaved.

The trial generally starts as a temptation to do a selfish thing that will let us continue in comfort and prosperity, or to stand by what is right and accept what seems sure to be poverty and failure. So powerful is the trial that, to those who are tempted, it plainly appears on the face of things that if they choose the low road, the baser option, their material success will be assured for the remainder of their lives, but if they do what is right, they'll be ruined forever.

Many people are appalled by what this path of wisdom seems to require of them, but they take the high road anyway. Then, as they withstand the temptation, the inner seducer, the small self, pretends to be an angel of light and whispers, "Think of those who depend upon you. Will you bring them down into disgrace and starvation?"

The strong and loving are those who overcome such trials. By not giving in to the urgings of the small self, they transform their minds and enter immediately into a higher realm of life, a higher vibration. Their spiritual eyes open to see the beautiful things that have always been there, just out of sight—and the poverty and ruin that seemed inevitable do not appear. Instead, a lasting success follows, with a peaceful heart and a quiet conscience.

But those who fail to overcome the temptations of the small self do not obtain the promised prosperity. Instead, their world displays to them their own lack of integrity. And since they've lost the high road, their hearts remain restless and their consciences troubled. The person who chooses the high road cannot ultimately fail; the wrong-doer, choosing the low road, cannot ultimately succeed, for as the great poet Sir Edwin Arnold wrote,

Such is the Law which moves to righteousness
Which none at last can turn aside or stay.

The heart of it is Love, the end of it
Is peace and consummation sweet—Obey![1]

Those who, fearing the loss of present pleasures or material comforts, deny this Law—and with it the Truth within themselves—can be injured, robbed, degraded, and trampled upon because they have already injured, robbed, degraded, and trampled upon their own higher selves. But those who hold to divine qualities and maintain an unblemished integrity cannot be subject to such conditions, because they've denied the cravings of the small self within them and taken refuge in Truth. The soul of integrity, the one who consistently chooses the high road, is beyond fear, failure, poverty, shame, and disgrace.

Slander, accusation, and malice cannot affect those who've annihilated the small self and risen above temptation. Nor can such apparent attacks get any bitter response from them—they don't even need to go about defending themselves to prove their innocence. Innocence and integrity alone answer all that hatred or hostility may attempt against them. Nor can they be affected by any apparent forces of darkness around them, having subdued all those forces within themselves. They turn all seemingly harmful things to good. Out of darkness, they bring light; out of hatred, love; out of dishonor, honor; and out of slander, appreciation and acceptance.[2] Any misrepresentations made about them only serve to make brighter the jewel of Truth within each and every one of them, glorifying their high and holy destinies.

Let those who've chosen the high road rejoice and be glad when they're severely tried, as did Buddha when tempted by Mara's demons under the Boddhi tree and Jesus when tempted in the wilderness. Let them be thankful that they've been given an opportunity to prove to themselves their commitment to the higher principles. Let them think, "Here's a spiritual opportunity! Though we may lose the whole world, that's just things that we've projected onto Creation! We choose the Truth, and with it, the vision to behold Creation itself!" In this way, they return good for harm and think compassionately of the wrongdoer.

Fear not. The slanderer, the backbiter, and the wrongdoer may seem to succeed for a time, but the divine Law of Justice prevails. The souls of integrity may seem to fail for a time, but they are invincible, and no weapon can be forged in any of the worlds, visible or invisible, that shall prevail against them. This is the victory of the peaceful warrior.

Essential Points

- There are times in the lives of everyone who has chosen to live from the ten divine qualities when their faith in and knowledge of those principles is tested to the utmost.
- The trial generally starts as a temptation to do a selfish thing that will let them continue in comfort and prosperity, or to do what is right and accept seemingly certain poverty and failure.
- Those who overcome such trials by not giving in to the urgings of the small self transform the mind; their spiritual eyes are opened and the poverty and ruin that seemed inevitable do not appear.

- Those who consistently choose the high road are beyond fear, failure, poverty, shame, and disgrace; slander, accusation, and malice cannot affect them.
- Those who choose the ten divine qualities' can rejoice and be glad when they're severely tried; they can be thankful for the opportunity to prove to themselves their commitment to the higher principle. In this way, they return good for harm and think compassionately of the wrongdoer.

6

DISCERNMENT

There is one skill fundamental to spiritual development: the ability to discern. Spiritual progress is painfully slow and uncertain until the eyes of discernment are opened, for without this testing, proving, searching ability, we grope in the dark, unable to distinguish the real from the unreal, the substance from the shadow, the false from the true. Without discernment, we too often mistake the inward promptings of our small self for the voice of the higher spirit of Truth.

A blind person in a new place may grope his or her way through darkness but not without a lot of confusion, many painful falls, and much bruising. Similarly, without discernment, people are mentally blind, and their lives consist of painful groping in the darkness—a confusion in which vice and virtue are indistinguishable from one another; where facts are taken for truths and opinions are confused with principles; and where ideas, events, people, and things appear to be unrelated to each other.

Ideally our minds and lives would be free from confusion. We can expect to be prepared to meet every mental, material, and spiritual difficulty and never be caught (as too many are) in the meshes of doubt, indecision, and uncertainty, even in the face of troubles and so-called misfortunes. We can be fortified against every emergency that can come against us. But such mental preparedness and strength cannot be attained without discernment, and discernment can only be developed by constantly exercising the mind.

The mind, like any muscle, is developed by use, and the constant exercise of the mind by continuously comparing and analyzing the ideas and opinions of others will develop and strengthen mental capacity and power. This is the function of a traditional education in the liberal arts—to train the mind in these abilities. Discernment, however, is something greater than the analytical and critical faculties; it's also a spiri - tual quality from which the cruelty and egotism that so often accompany criticism are eliminated and we see things as they are, not as we would like them—or as we were trained to expect them—to be.

Discernment, being a spiritual skill, can only be developed by spiritual methods, namely by questioning, examining, and analyzing one's own ideas, opinions, and conduct. Our critical, fault-finding tendencies must no longer be applied to the opinions and conduct of others but to our own self—with no holds barred. We must be prepared to question every one of our own opinions, thoughts, and behaviors and test them against our chosen principles, the ten divine qualities listed on page 61. To "prove all things" (1 Thessalonians 5:21) is to find the useful ideas and cast the garbage aside. Only in this way can the discernment that destroys confusion be developed.

However, before we can begin such mental exercise, we must become teachable. This does *not* mean we have to allow ourselves to be led by others. It *does* mean that we're ready to observe our thoughts and feelings and then let go of any once-cherished thoughts, beliefs, assumptions, or opinions that have no logical basis or would get in the way of our accomplishing our highest dreams.

Anyone who says, "I'm right!" without being willing to question his or her position will remain stuck in prejudice and will not acquire discernment. But people who humbly ask, "Am I right?" and then proceed to test and prove their positions by earnest thought and the love of Truth will always be able to discover the true and distinguish it from the false or unworthy. They will have the priceless power of discernment.

Those who are afraid to question their opinions or reason out their positions will have to develop moral courage before they can acquire discernment. They must be fearless with themselves before they can perceive the clear principles of Truth and receive its all-revealing light. They need not fear; Truth cannot suffer under examination and analysis; the more it's questioned, the brighter it shines. By contrast, the more error is questioned, the darker it grows; it can't survive searching thought.

Confusion, suffering,
and spiritual darkness follow the thoughtless.
Harmony, blessedness, and the Light of Truth
attend upon the thoughtful.
Passion and prejudice are blind and cannot discriminate . . .

Those who reason and meditate learn to be mindful, and those who can discern discover the eternally True.

Essential Points

• Without discernment, we too often mistake the inward promptings of our small self for the voice of the higher spirit of Truth. With discernment we can be fortified against every emergency that can come against us.
• Discernment, being a spiritual skill, can only be developed by questioning, examining, and analyzing one's own ideas, opinions, and conduct, and testing them against our chosen principles.
• Anyone who says, "I'm right!" without being willing to question his or her position will remain stuck in prejudice and will not acquire discernment.
• Those who reason and meditate learn to be mindful, and those who can discern discover the eternally True.

7

BELIEF: THE BASIS OF ACTION

B elief is an important word in the teachings of the wise, and it figures prominently in all religions. In the Christian tradition, for example, a certain kind of belief is necessary to experience salvation or rebirth, and the Buddha definitely taught that accessing one's beliefs is the first and most essential step in the way of Truth, for without noble belief there can be no compassionate action. Those who haven't learned how to govern their beliefs have not yet understood the simplest elements of Truth.

Belief, as defined by the great spiritual teachers, is not belief in any particular school, philosophy, or religion but the attitude of mind that forms the basis of one's life. Jesus, especially, taught that our experiences are a function of our belief: "It shall be done to you according to your belief" (Matthew 9:29). Belief and experience are inseparable, for the former determines the latter.

Belief is the basis of all action, and the belief that dominates the heart or mind is shown in the outer life. Everyone acts, thinks, and lives according to the beliefs rooted in their innermost being, and the nature of the law that governs the mind is such that it's absolutely impossible for anyone to believe in two opposing conditions at the same time. It's impossible, for instance, to believe in justice *and* injustice, hatred *and* love, peace *and* strife, the small self *and* Truth. Everyone fundamentally believes in one or the other of these opposites—never in both—and their daily conduct indicates which side of the fence they're on.[1]

The people who believe in Justice as a universal power, who regard it as an eternal and indestructible principle, never boil with righteous indignation, are never cynical and pessimistic over the inequalities of life, and remain calm and untroubled through all trials and difficulties. It's impossible for them to act otherwise, for they believe that justice reigns and that injustice is fleeting and illusory. From all accounts, George Washington was such a man, as are Nelson Mandela and Archbishop Desmond Tutu in South Africa, and Aung San Suu Kyi, the voice of freedom in Myanmar (formerly Burma).

People who are often enraged over the injustices of their fellow human beings, who talk about being treated badly, or who mourn over the lack of justice in the world around them show through their conduct and mental attitude that they believe in injustice. They may protest to the contrary, but in their inmost hearts they believe that confusion and chaos are dominant in the universe, and as a result, their conduct is faulty and they dwell in a world of misery and unrest.

Again, those who believe in Love, in its stability and power, practice it under all circumstances. They never deviate from it and bestow it upon friends and enemies alike. Mother Teresa and Francis of Assisi are examples of such believers. Those who slander and condemn, belittle others, or regard them with contempt believe not in Love but in its opposite. All their actions prove it, even though with tongue or pen they may glowingly praise love.

Believers in Peace are known by their peaceful conduct. It's impossible for them to engage in strife. If attacked, they do not retaliate, for they have seen the majesty of the angel of Peace and can no longer pay homage to the demon of strife. The great liberator of India, Gandhi, was called *Mahatma*, "Great Soul," because he was such a believer. In contrast, the lovers of strife and argument, those who rush into self-defense upon any or every provocation, believe in strife and will have nothing to do with Peace.

Those who believe in Truth renounce their own small selves—that is, they refuse to center their lives in those self-justifications, desires, and characteristics that crave only their own gratification. By putting these selfish things aside, they become steadfastly fixed in Truth and live wise, beautiful, and blameless lives. In *The Autobiography of Benjamin Franklin*, Franklin describes how he went about renouncing a vice-ridden youth; Gandhi does the same in his autobiography, *The Story of My Experiments with Truth*. The believers in self, on the other hand, are known by their daily indulgences, gratifications, and vanities and by the disappointment, sorrow, and humiliation they continually suffer, which is the stuff of novels and dramas aplenty.

> *The believers in Truth do not suffer;*
> *They have given up that self which is the*
> *cause of such suffering.*

There are two ways to describe how the universe works: as permanent and eternal principles directing human life toward law and harmony, or as the opposite of these principles, which leads to chaos in life and in the world. Most people believe in some mixture of the two.

Belief in the divine principles of Justice, Compassion, and Love constitute what's called "right belief," laid down by the Buddha as being the basis of "right conduct." These are two of the steps on the Buddha's eightfold Noble Path. This belief is also the belief that leads to salvation according to the Christian scriptures. In both traditions, those who so believe build their whole lives upon these principles and, in the process, purify their hearts and perfect their lives.

Belief in the opposite of these divine principles constitutes what religions call "unbelief," and this unbelief is manifested as a troubled and imperfect life. Islam is based on this principle of belief vs. unbelief, with its constant admonition that "there is no god but Allah" ("Allah" being the Arabic word describing the divine Source of all that is) and that "unbelievers" bring about their own demise.[2] Where there is total belief in the divine principles, in whatever religious tradition, there is a blameless and perfect life. Where there is unbelief there is suffering and sorrow, the mind and life are improperly governed, and there is affliction and distress: "By their fruits ye shall know them" (Matthew 7:16).

Today there's much talk about "Christ consciousness," but what does this mean? It must mean absolute belief in the principles that Jesus the Christ and all the other great spiritual teachers of humanity enunciated and lived. Those who declare a belief in higher consciousness and still choose to live in lust and indulgence, or in the spirit of hostility and condemnation, are self-deceived. They don't really believe in higher consciousness; they believe only in their own small, egoic selves.

As a faithful servant delights in carrying out the commands of a beloved master, so do those who believe in higher consciousness follow the lessons of the great spiritual teachers. This is the test the Apostle John described when he said, "The one who says, 'I know him [Jesus],' and keeps not his commandments, is a liar, and the Truth is not in that person. But whoever keeps his word, in them is the Word of God truly perfected" (1 John 2:5). They are free and we can see it.

On careful analysis it's clear that belief lies at the root of all human conduct. Every thought, every act, every habit is the direct outcome of a certain fixed belief, and one's conduct alters only as one's beliefs are modified. This is why Jesus could say "It shall be as you believe."

Declaring a theological creed or belief is useless, for what good can it do for people to state that Jesus died for the sins of the world, or that Jesus is God, or that people are "justified by faith" (Romans 5:1–2) if they continue to live from the demeaning qualities of their small self? All we need to ask is this: "How do we live? How do we conduct ourselves in trying circumstances?" The answer will show whether we believe in the power of evil or the power of Good.

What we cling to, we believe; what we practice, we believe. When our belief in something ceases, we can no longer cling to or practice it; it falls away from us like worn-out clothing. People cling to their lusts, lies, and vanities because they believe there is gain and happiness in them. When they transfer their belief to the divine qualities with clarity and humility, those past beliefs trouble them no more.

People are saved from error and its effects in their lives by their belief in the supremacy of Truth. Jesus said, "You shall know Truth and Truth shall make you free" (John 8:32). They are freed from sin, which is simply "missing the mark" or "straying from the path," by their belief in holiness (a word coming from the root "wholeness") or Perfection.[3] They are saved from harm by belief in omnipresent Good, for every belief is manifested in every life.

Those who believe in Good live spiritual and godly lives. As Jesus suggested in the gospels, they are gods themselves, for goodness is one of the names of God, and these godly minds leave behind them all sins and sorrows, replacing them with steadfast and unwavering faith in the Supreme Good.

Essential Points

- Belief and experience are inseparable, for the former determines the latter.
- Belief, as defined by the great spiritual teachers, is not belief in any particular school, philosophy, or religion but the attitude of mind that forms the basis of one's life.
- Those who live in lust and indulgence, or in the spirit of hostility and condemnation, do not believe in higher consciousness; they believe only in their own small, egoic selves.
- What we cling to, we believe; what we practice, we believe. When our belief in something ceases, we can no longer cling to or practice it.
- "How do we live? How do we conduct ourselves in trying circumstances?" The answer will show whether we believe in the power of evil or the power of Good.

8

THE SAVING BELIEF

It's been said that our lives and characters are the outcome of our beliefs. It has also been said that our beliefs have nothing whatsoever to do with our lives. Both statements are true. The confusion and contradiction of these two statements are only apparent, and they're quickly dispelled when we remember that there are two entirely distinct kinds of beliefs, namely head-belief and heart-belief.

Head-belief, or intellectual belief, is not fundamental and causative but superficial and resulting, and it has no power in molding a person's character, as anyone can easily see. Take, for instance, half a dozen people from any particular creed. They may hold the same theological beliefs and confess the same articles of faith, yet their characters are vastly different. One will be just as noble as another is ignoble; one will be mild and gentle, another coarse and irascible; one will be honest, another dishonest; one will indulge certain habits that another will rigidly avoid; and so on, plainly indicating that theological beliefs aren't significant factors in their lives.

Our theological beliefs are merely our intellectual opinions or views of the universe—God, the Bible, Buddhist sutras, the Tao, the Koran, and so forth. Behind and beneath these head-beliefs lie the hidden, silent, secret beliefs of our hearts, which are deeply rooted in our innermost beings. These beliefs are what mold and make our whole lives, and they're what make those half-dozen people with the same theology vary so widely in their deeds—they differ in the vital belief of their hearts.

So what is heart-belief? Our heart-belief is what we love, cling to and foster—and believing and loving it, we practice it. This is how our lives are affected by our beliefs. Notice, though, that it has no relation to the particular creed that comprises our intellectual beliefs. People cling to toxic and immoral things because they believe in them; others do not cling to them because they've ceased to believe in them. We can't cling to anything unless we believe in it. Belief always precedes action. Therefore, as we've already seen, our deeds and lives are the fruits of our beliefs.

Recall the priest and the Levite in the New Testament parable of the Good Samaritan. They both passed by the injured and helpless man. They no doubt held very strongly to the theological doctrines of their fathers—that was their intellectual belief—but in their hearts they did not believe in mercy, and so lived and acted accordingly. The Good Samaritan, on the other hand, may or may not have had any theological beliefs, nor was it necessary that he should have; but in his heart he believed in mercy and acted accordingly.

Strictly speaking, there is one saving belief that vitally affects life, and it is our heart-belief. Those who believe with their hearts in all things good will love and live in them, and those who believe in things that are toxic and selfish will love and cling to them. The tree is known by its fruits.

So our beliefs about God or religion are just head-beliefs and of no consequence. Since our lives are bound up in our heart-beliefs, we can see that the thoughts we harbor, our attitude of mind toward others, and our actions determine and demonstrate whether the beliefs of our hearts are fixed in the false or true.

Essential Points

- Head-belief, or intellectual belief is not fundamental and causative but superficial and resulting, and it has no power in the molding of a person's character.

- Behind and beneath these head-beliefs lie the hidden, silent, secret beliefs of our hearts. These beliefs mold and make our whole lives, and they're what make people with the same theology vary so widely in their deeds.
- Those who believe with their hearts in all things good will love and live in them, and those who believe in those things that are toxic and selfish will love and cling to them.

9

THOUGHT AND ACTION

As fruit is to the tree and water is to the spring, so is action to thought. The fruit of the tree and the gushing of the spring from the rock are both the effect of a combination of natural processes in nature that have long worked together unseen to produce the phenomenon. Just so, the beautiful acts of enlightenment and the dark deeds of evildoing are both the ripened effects of trains of thought that have long been harbored in the mind. It doesn't come into manifestation suddenly and without a cause; it's the result of a long and silent growth, the end of a hidden process that has long been gathering force.

Once we are aware of this hidden process of thought, we can see that it's neither sudden nor causeless when people who were believed, and probably believed themselves, to have stood firm in the divine qualities were greatly tempted and fall into a bad habit or some grievous act. The falling was merely the end, the finished result, of what has long developed in the mind.

These people have permitted toxic thoughts to enter their minds. It may have been through a book or paper, a television show or conversation, or in a song they've appreciated the melody and rhythm of. After the second and third encounters, they've allowed the thoughts to nestle in their hearts.

Gradually these people became accustomed to these thoughts and cherished and tended them by focusing on them, repeating them, listening or reading about them, and exploring their possibilities—often by the seemingly innocent wondering and asking about why these thoughts were in their lives. So the toxic thoughts grew, until at last they attained such strength and force that they attracted to themselves the opportunity that enabled them to burst forth and ripen into acts. Just like the stately building whose foundations have been gradually undermined by the action of waterfalls, so at last the strong fall who have allowed corrupt thoughts to creep into their minds and secretly undermine their characters.

When we see that all immorality and temptation are the natural outcome of one's thoughts, the way to overcome them becomes plain; its achievement becomes a near possibility and a certain reality sooner or later if we only admit, cherish, wonder about, and brood upon thoughts that are loving and good. These thoughts, just as surely as the toxic ones, will grow and gather force and at last attract to themselves the opportunities that will enable them to ripen into acts.

The New Testament tells us "there is nothing hidden that shall not be revealed," and every thought that is harbored in the mind must, by virtue of the impelling force that is inherent in the universe, at last blossom into a good or bad act according to its nature.[1] The divine teacher and the sensualist are both the product of their own thoughts. They're ordinary people who've become what they are as the result of the seeds of thought they have planted or allowed to fall into the garden of their hearts and have afterwards watered, tended, and cultivated.

Let no one think that he or she can overcome immorality and temptation by wrestling with them when they appear in life. We can only overcome them by focusing our thoughts. We must follow the process that Brother Lawrence calls "practicing the presence."[2] If we will, every day, in the silence of our souls and in the performance of our duties, work to overcome all inclinations away from the ten divine qualities and put in their place only thoughts that will endure the light, then the opportunity to do harm will not appear. It must give place to opportunity for accomplishing good, for we can only attract that which is in harmony with our natures, and no temptation can gravitate to us unless there is a thought in our hearts capable of responding to it.

So guard well your thoughts, reader, for what you really are in your secret thoughts today, be it good or evil, you will become in actual deed sooner or later. Those who unwearyingly guard the portals of their minds against the intrusion of toxic, weak, or malignant thoughts and occupy themselves with loving thoughts—with joyful, strong, and beautiful thoughts—will bring forth the fruits of gentle and holy deeds when the season of their ripening comes, and no temptation can come against them.

Essential Points

- The beautiful acts of enlightenment and the dark deeds of evildoing are both the ripened effects of trains of thought that have long been harbored in the mind.

- Toxic thoughts enter minds through a book or paper, television show, conversation, or a song. They nestle in hearts, and people gradually became accustomed to these thoughts and tend them by focusing on them. So the toxic thoughts grow until they ripen into acts.

- If we only admit, cherish, wonder about, and brood upon thoughts that are loving and good, those thoughts, just as surely as the toxic ones, will grow and gather force and at last attract to themselves the opportunities which will enable them to ripen into act.

- If we will, every day, in the silence of our souls and in the performance of our duties, work to overcome all inclinations away from the ten divine qualities and put in their place only thoughts that will endure the light, then the opportunity to do harm will not appear.

10

YOUR MENTAL ATTITUDE

As a being of thought, your dominant mental attitude determines your condition in life. It's also the gauge of your knowledge and the measure of your accomplishment. The so-called limitations of your nature are simply the boundary lines of your thoughts; they are self-erected fences, and they can be drawn into a narrower circle, allowed to remain static, or extended to a wider sphere.

You are the thinker of your thoughts, and as such, you are the maker of yourself and your condition. Thought is causal and creative, and it appears in your character and life; there are no accidents. Your life's harmonies and distress are the responsive echoes of your thoughts. As you think, your life appears.

If your dominant mental attitude is peaceable and lovable, bliss and blessedness will follow you; if it is resistant and hostile, trouble and distress will cloud your path.

Out of ill will comes grief and disaster.
Out of goodwill, healing and reparation.

You may imagine that your circumstances are separate from you, but they're directly related to your world of thoughts. Nothing appears without an adequate cause. Everything that happens is just and equitable. Nothing is fated; everything is formed.

As you think, you travel; as you love, you attract. You are today where your thoughts have brought you; you will be tomorrow where your thoughts take you. You can't escape the result of your thoughts, but you can endure and learn; you can accept and be glad.

You will always come to the place where your most abiding and intense thought—what you love most—can be fully gratified. If what you love is sleazy or foul, you will come to a sleazy or foul place; if it's beautiful, you'll come to a beautiful place. You can alter your thoughts and so alter your condition.

You are powerful, not powerless! You are as powerful to obey as you are to disobey; as strong to be loving as to be hostile; as ready for wisdom as for ignorance. You can learn what you will or remain as ignorant as you choose. If you love knowledge, you will obtain it; if you love wisdom, you will secure it; and if you love clarity, you will realize it. All things await your acceptance, and you choose them by the thoughts you entertain.

We are wise because we love wisdom and choose wise thoughts; people remain ignorant because they love ignorance and choose ignorant thoughts. No one is hindered by another; we are only hindered by ourselves. And no one suffers because of another; we suffer only because of ourselves. Strive to perceive the vastness and grandeur of your responsibility. By the noble gateway of loving thoughts, you can enter the highest consciousness; by the ignoble doorway of toxic thoughts, you can descend into the lowest hell.

Your mental attitude toward others will faithfully react upon you and manifest itself in every relation of your life. Every hostile and selfish thought you send out comes back to you in your circumstances in some form of suffering; every loving and unselfish thought returns to you in some form of blessedness.

When you know yourself, you'll see that every event in your life is perfectly balanced with your thoughts. When you understand the law within your mind, you'll stop describing yourself as the powerless and blind victim of circumstance and will become the strong and seeing ruler of your life.

Essential Points

- As a being of thought, your dominant mental attitude will determine your condition in life.
- If your dominant mental attitude is peaceable and lovable, bliss and blessedness will follow you; if it's resistant and hostile, trouble and distress will cloud your path.
- You will always come to the place where your most abiding and intense thought can be fully gratified. If you love knowledge, you will obtain it; if you love wisdom, you will secure it; and if you love clarity, you will realize it.
- No one is hindered by another; we are only hindered by ourselves. And no one suffers because of another; we suffer only because of ourselves.
- Every event in your life is perfectly balanced with your thoughts.

11

SOWING AND REAPING

Travel to the fields and country lanes in the springtime and you will see farmers and gardeners busy sowing seeds in the newly prepared soil. If you stopped and asked any of them what kind of produce they expected to grow from the seeds they were sowing, they'd look at you funny and tell you they weren't "expecting" at all. They would tell you that it's common sense that their produce will be what they're sowing—wheat or barley or turnips, as the case may be—and that they sow their crops for the very purpose of reproducing that particular one.

Every fact and process in nature contains a moral lesson for those who would see it, for there is no law in the physical world that doesn't operate with the same certainty in our minds and lives. Across the spiritual traditions, many parables illustrate this truth, being drawn from the simple facts of nature.

Thoughts, words, and acts are seeds sown, and by the inviolable law of things, they produce the kind of life they promise. Those thinking hostile thoughts bring hatred upon themselves; those thinking loving thoughts are loved. The person whose thoughts, words, and actions are sincere is surrounded by sincere friends, while the one who is insincere is surrounded by insincere people.

Those who sow wrong thoughts and deeds and then pray that God will bless them are in the position of a farmer who, having sown weed seeds, asks God to bring forth a harvest of wheat.[1]

That which ye sow, ye reap. See yonder fields!
The sesame was sesame,
The corn was corn.
The silence and the darkness knew!
So is a man's fate born.[2]

We become reapers of the things we sow. Those who would be blessed, let them scatter blessings. Those who would be happy, let them help cultivate the happiness of others.

Then there's another side to this seed sowing. Farmers must scatter most of their seeds upon the land and leave them to the elements in order to eventually harvest this crop. Were they to hoard their seeds, they would not grow their produce and their seeds would lose vitality, dry up, and die. The seed dies when the farmer sows it, most certainly, but in the right place, it brings forth a great abundance. So in life, we get by giving; we grow rich by scattering gratitude and blessings. Those who say they have knowledge they can't share because the world is incapable of receiving it either don't really have it or, if they do possess it, they'll soon be deprived of it. To hoard is to lose; to keep exclusively is to be dispossessed.

Even those who want to increase their material wealth must be willing to part with and invest what capital they have first. So as long as they hold on to their precious money, they will not only remain poor but grow poorer every day. They will, after all, lose the thing they love, and will lose it without increase. But if they wisely let it go—if they scatter their seeds of gold like the farmers sow their seeds—then they can faithfully wait for, and reasonably expect, the increase.

Some continually ask God to give them peace and purity, righteousness and blessedness, but they never get them. Why not? Because they're not practicing them, not sowing them. I once heard a preacher pray very earnestly for forgiveness, and shortly afterwards, in the course of his sermon, he called upon his congregation to "show no mercy to the enemies of the church." Such self-delusion is pitiful, but some have yet to learn that the way to obtain peace and blessedness is to scatter peaceful and blessed thoughts, words, and deeds.

Some believe that they can sow the seeds of strife, lack of clarity, and faithlessness and then gather in a rich harvest of peace, clarity, and harmony by merely asking for it. What more pathetic sight than to see an irritable and argumentative person praying for peace. We reap what we sow, and we can reap all blessedness now and at once if we just put aside selfishness and sow the seeds of kindness, gentleness, and love.

If you're feeling troubled, perplexed, sorrowful, or unhappy, ask yourself:

- "What mental seeds have I been sowing?"
- "Are they seeds of trouble and sorrow or gratitude and love?"
- "What is my attitude toward others?"
- "What have I done for my friends and family?"
- "Am I reaping joyous fruits from my beliefs, thoughts, and actions toward others, or am I reaping bitter weeds?"

Seek within and you shall find—and, having found, abandon all the seeds of the small self and sow only the seeds of Truth from this moment forward. Just look to the farmers and gardeners to see the simple truth of this wisdom.

Essential Points

- Those who sow wrong thoughts and deeds and pray that God will bless them are in the position of a farmer who, having sown weed seeds, asks God to bring forth a harvest of wheat.
- We get by giving; we grow rich by scattering gratitude and blessings. Those who would be blessed, let them scatter blessings. Those who would be happy, let them help cultivate the happiness of others.

12

THE REIGN OF LAW

The once-honored god of revenge, hostility, and jealousy who gloats over the downfall of enemies; the partial god who gratifies all our narrow and selfish desires; the god of exclusiveness and favoritism who saves only the creatures of a particular special creed—such were the gods of our soul's infancy. They are the fabrications of the selfish small self within each of us, gods as base and foolish as our lesser selves. These petty little gods have had their day. They are, after all, mere creatures of human caprice and ignorance who have been quarreled over for centuries but have now fallen out of favor. Their defenders have grown weary of the strife, and now, everywhere, they are relinquishing and breaking up these helpless idols of their long worship.

The story of their dethronement begins with Abraham, continues through Moses' training of his people in the wilderness, is the core of the Hanukkah story, and reaches its pinnacle in the revelation to Mohammed the Blessed, who saw that the idols worshipped in Mecca had no power in the presence of the One Source, called *Allah* in Arabic.

Though these petty gods may have been relinquished with bitter tears and misgivings and their idols broken with bleeding hands, we held fast and did not lose sight of Truth. And in the process, we drew nearer to the great, silent Heart of Love. Destroying the idols of the small self, we began to experience power that cannot be destroyed and entered into a wider knowledge of Love, Peace, and Joy—a state in which revenge and partiality cannot exist. We became the light from whose presence the darkness of fear, doubt, and selfishness flee.

The world has reached an age that has witnessed the passing of the false gods, the gods of selfishness and illusion. Humanity has lost faith in a god who can be cajoled, who rules arbitrarily and capriciously and subverts the whole order of things to gratify the wishes of worshippers. Instead, we are turning, with a new sparkle in our eyes and joy in our hearts, to the new but ancient revelation that has again dawned upon the world. We are experiencing a realization of one universal, impersonal Supreme Law of Being, the light of which strikes fear in the perishable gods taking shelter under the shadow of the small self.

And to that Law we turn, not for personal happiness and gratification, which are fleeting, but for knowledge, for understanding, for wisdom, for liberation from the bondage of the small self. And we do not seek in vain, nor are we sent away empty and frustrated.

As has been clear throughout this text, we find within ourselves the working of the Law, so that every thought, impulse, act, and word brings about a result in exact accordance with its own nature. Thoughts of love bring about beautiful and blissful conditions; hostile thoughts bring about distorted and painful conditions. Thoughts and actions both good and harmful are weighed in the faultless balance of this Law, and they receive their equal measure of blessedness on one hand, and misery on the other.

After realizing this Law, we can then enter a new path of life, one on which we no longer accuse, doubt, fret, or lose hope, for we know that the universal Law is right, the cosmos is right, and that if wrong exists at all in our world, it must be we ourselves who are wrong. Our salvation depends upon us, our own efforts, our personal acceptance of all that is good, and our deliberate rejection of all that is harmful. We become doers of the Truth, and in so doing, acquire knowledge, grow in wisdom, and enter into the glorious life of liberation from the bondage of the small self.

The Law is perfect; it enlightens the eyes. Imperfection lies in ignorance, in blind folly. So Perfection, which is knowledge of the Law, is ready for all who earnestly seek it. It belongs to the order of things—it's yours and mine now if we would only put self-seeking aside and focus on the divine qualities.

The knowledge of Truth, with its unspeakable joy, its calmness, and quiet strength, is not for those who persist in clinging to their "rights," defending their "interests," and fighting for their "opinions." Their works are permeated with the personal "I" and built upon the shifting sands of selfishness and egotism. Those who renounce these causes of strife, these sources of pain and sorrow, are, indeed, children of Truth, disciples of the most High.

These children of Truth are in the world today; they are thinking, acting, writing, and speaking. Even prophets are among us, and their influence is pervading the whole earth. They are at work in offices, factories, schools, churches and temples, and stores. They participate in study groups, write books and blogs, gather with friends, and can be heard and seen on certain television and radio shows. Because of their inner work and external presence, an undercurrent of global joy is gathering force in the world as people everywhere are moved to new aspirations and hopes, and even those who can neither see nor hear still feel within themselves strange yearnings after a better and fuller life.

The Law reigns in the hearts and lives of those who have come to understand its reign,

Who have sought out the tabernacle of Truth by the pathway of unselfishness.

The Law does not alter for us; if it did, it would mean that the perfect must become imperfect. Instead, we alter for the Law—we, the imperfect, must (which is to say, we can't not) become perfect. The Law cannot be broken. We must (again, we can't not) obey it in accordance with harmony, order, and justice. Just as we can't not obey the law of gravity, we can't avoid obeying this universal Law.

And, as obedience to the Law leads to the dissolution of the small self, it brings unclouded joy and undying peace, while clinging to one's selfish inclinations brings clouds of pain and sorrow, which darken the Light of Truth, shutting out all real blessedness.

We can see, then, that there's no more painful bondage than being at the mercy of one's selfish inclinations, and no greater liberty than complete obedience to the Law. And the Law is that, ultimately, the heart *shall* be purified, the mind regenerated, and the whole being brought in alignment with Love until the small self no longer runs our lives. Then our joy is everlasting and Love is all in all.

Ah, beautiful Truth!
To know that now we may accept our divine heritage
and enter the Light of Wisdom!
Oh, pitiful error! To reject it because of love of self!

Truly, the Law reigns and does so forever, and Justice and Love are its eternal ministers. For the reign of Law is the reign of Love, and Love waits for all, rejecting none. In fact, Love may be claimed and entered into now, for it is the heritage of all.

Essential Points

- The world has reached an age that has witnessed the passing of the false gods, the gods of selfishness and illusion.
- Instead, we turn to the Supreme Law of Being, not for personal happiness and gratification, which are fleeting, but for knowledge, for understanding, for wisdom, for liberation from the bondage of the small self.
- After realizing this Law, we can then enter a new path of life, one on which we no longer accuse, doubt, fret, or lose hope.
- Those who renounce these causes of strife, these sources of pain and sorrow, are, indeed, children of Truth, disciples of the most High,

and they're in the world today; they're thinking, acting, writing, and speaking, and their influence is pervading the whole earth.

- The reign of Law is the reign of Love, and Love waits for all, rejecting none. In fact, love may be claimed and entered into now, for it is the heritage of all.

13

THE SUPREME JUSTICE

The material universe is maintained and preserved by the balance of its forces. Similarly, the spiritual universe is sustained and protected by the perfect balance of its equivalents. As in the physical world, nature abhors a vacuum, so in the spiritual world disharmony cannot be maintained. As an eternal and perfect mathematical symmetry underlies all the disturbances and destructions of nature and the many permutations of its forms, so at the heart of life, behind all its pain, uncertainty, and unrest, the eternal harmony and unbroken peace of the inviolable Supreme Justice can be found.

Is there, then, no injustice in the universe? There is injustice and there is not; it depends on the kind of life and the state of consciousness from which we look at the world and judge. Those who live unjustly see injustice everywhere; those who have overcome the justifications of the small, egoic self see the operations of justice in every aspect of human life. Injustice is the confused, feverish dream of the small self, real enough to those who are dreaming it; Justice is the permanent reality in life, gloriously visible to those who have awakened from the painful nightmare of the small self's imaginings.

The divine order of the cosmos can't be perceived until self-justification and self-protection are transcended; the Supreme Justice can't be experienced until all sense of injury and wrong is consumed in the pure flames of faultless, all-embracing Love.

Those who think, "I've been slighted, injured, and insulted" or "I've been treated unjustly," can't know what Justice is. Blinded by the imaginings of the small self, they can't perceive the clear principles of Truth, and brooding on the wrongs they feel have been done to them, they live in continual misery.

In general, where compulsive passions and justification of the small self seem to reign, a ceaseless conflict of forces causes suffering for all who are involved in them; there is action and reaction, deed and consequence, cause and effect. This is the stuff of novels, action films, and television dramas.

All the while, within and above all, the Supreme Justice regulates this play of forces with the utmost mathematical accuracy, balancing cause and effect with the finest precision. But this divine Justice is not perceived by those who are engaged in the conflict. No one can perceive it until the fierce warfare of compulsive passion is left behind.

The world of self-justification and compulsive passion is one of wars, quarreling, schisms, lawsuits, accusations, condemnations, faults, weaknesses, follies, hostility, revenge, and resentment. How can we perceive Justice or understand Truth if we're even partly involved in these? No one caught in the flames of a burning building can sit down right then and there and reason out the cause of the fire!

In this realm of self-justification, people see injustice in the actions of others because, seeing only immediate appearances, they regard every act as standing by itself, undetached from cause and consequence. Having no knowledge of cause and effect in the spiritual sphere, they don't see the precise balancing process unfolding, nor do they ever regard their own actions as unjust—only the actions of others.

For example, an activist, seeking justice and peace for all, takes part in a demonstration in the town square. The local police, afraid that the assembly will become a riot, implement crowd-control measures. The crowd, frustrated that their rights to assemble are being impinged upon, lean on the police's control measures. The police, seeing their fears become manifest, upgrade their measures from fences and shields to batons, tear gas, and fire hoses. The activist becomes enraged by the injustice of their actions and strikes out, being injured and hauled off to jail in the process. Later, he sues the police for impinging on his rights and injuring him in the course of "peaceful assembly." Each of the people along the path of pain and suffering thinks of themselves as acting humanely and the others to be unjust and cruel, but they are only teaching the wrong lesson to the world and themselves.

This kind of ignorance keeps hostility and strife alive, as people living in anger and resentment blindly inflict suffering upon themselves, not finding the true way in life. Hatred is met with hatred, strife with strife. People who kill others kill themselves; thieves who live by depriving others are themselves deprived; the predator that preys on others is hunted and killed; the accuser is accused, the condemner condemned, and the denouncer denounced. "Such is the Law," Sir Edwin Arnold writes,

> By this the slayer's knife doth stab himself;
> The unjust judge has lost his own defender;
> The false tongue dooms its lie; the creeping thief
> And spoiler rob to render.[1]

There are active and passive sides to life. Fraud and fool, oppressor and slave, aggressor and retaliator, the charlatan and the superstitious—all complement each other and come together by the operation of Justice. People unconsciously cooperate in the mutual production of their own affliction: "The blind lead the blind . . . [and] both fall together into the ditch" (Luke 6:39). Pain, grief, sorrow, and misery are the fruits when self-justification is the flower.

Where the self-justifying soul sees only injustice, those who have conquered self-justification see only cause and effect; they see the Supreme Justice at work. It's impossible for such souls to experience injustice, because they've ceased to see it. They know that no one can injure or cheat them because they no longer injure or cheat themselves.

However passionately or ignorantly other people may act toward us, they can't possibly cause us pain, for whatever comes to us, whether it be abuse and persecution or health and happiness, comes as the effect of what we ourselves have sent out. It's best, therefore, to regard all things as good, rejoice in all things, love our enemies, and bless those who curse us, for these poor, blind souls are simply instruments, helping us restore our balance in the great Law. This teaching is the essence of the Beatitudes and the social doctrines of most spiritual traditions.

Only when all resentment, retaliation, self-seeking, and egotism are put away can we arrive at a state of equilibrium in which we can tune in to the eternal and universal Equilibrium. Then, having lifted ourselves above our fixations, we're like the solitary dweller upon a mountain who looks down upon the conflict of the storms below. We can understand them and contemplate them with a calm and penetrating insight. For this sage, injustice has ceased; there is only ignorance and suffering on one hand and enlightenment and bliss on the other. Those who have become wise see not only that fools and slaves need sympathy but that the fraudulent and oppressors are equally in need of it, and so compassion is extended toward all.

> *The Supreme Justice and the Supreme Love are one.*
> *Cause and effect cannot be avoided.*
> *Consequences cannot be escaped.*

Those who give in to hostility, resentment, anger, and condemnation are subject to injustice just as the dreamer is subject to the dream, and they can see only injustice. But those who have overcome those fiery elements of the self know that unerring Justice presides over all—that in reality there is no such thing as injustice in the whole of the universe.

Essential Points

- At the heart of life, behind all its pain, uncertainty, and unrest, abides the eternal harmony and unbroken peace of the inviolable Supreme Justice.

- Those who live unjustly see injustice everywhere; those who have overcome their tendencies toward self-justification see the operations of justice in every aspect of human life.
- Those who give in to hostility, resentment, anger, and condemnation are subject to injustice just as the dreamer is subject to the dream, and they can only see injustice.
- Those with no knowledge of cause and effect in the spiritual sphere don't see the precise balancing process unfolding, nor do they ever regard their own actions as unjust—only the actions of others.
- Only when all resentment, retaliation, self-seeking, and egotism are put away can we arrive at a state of equilibrium from which to tune in to the eternal and universal Equilibrium.

14

THE USE OF REASON

Some have said that reason is a blind guide drawing us away from Truth, rather than leading us to it. If that were so, it would be best to be unreasonable and to persuade others to do so. The great spiritual teachers have found, however, that developing the divine faculty of reason brings calm and mental poise, helping us to cheerfully meet the problems and difficulties of life.

In fact, without the aid of reason, Truth cannot be experienced, and those who refuse to light the lamp of reason will never perceive the Light of Truth, for the light of reason is a reflection of that greater Light.

Reason is a purely abstract quality that comes midway between our animal nature and divine consciousness. It leads, if used well, from darkness to the Light. It's true that reason may be enlisted in the service of the lower, self-seeking nature, but this is only when it's applied partially and imperfectly. A fuller development of reason leads away from the selfish nature and ultimately allies us with the divine qualities.

Some spiritual seekers are following the fabled knight Percival who, searching for the Holy Grail of Truth and the life of perfection, is again and again, as Tennyson says, "left alone, and wearying in a land of sand and thorns."[1] The seekers are not stranded there because they've followed reason but because they still cling to, and are reluctant to leave behind, some remnants of their lower natures.

Those who use the light of reason as a torch to search for Truth will not be left in comfortless darkness.

> *Come now, let us reason together, said the Lord; though your sins be as scarlet, they shall be as white as snow.* (Isaiah 1:18)

All who would exchange the scarlet robe of wickedness and suffering for the white garment of blamelessness and peace must use their reason freely, fully, and faithfully. Sadly, though, too many people pass through untold sufferings in their lives and die with their blind convictions because they refuse to reason; they cling to dark delusions that even a faint glimmer of the light of reason would dispel.

Those who've proved and know these truths realize that we must find another way; we must

> *tread the middle road, whose course*
> *Bright reason traces,*
> *and soft quiet smooths.* [2]

Reason leads away from self-justification and selfishness into the quiet ways of sweet persuasion and gentle forgiveness.

Many people maintain the strange delusion that reason is somehow connected with the denial of God's existence. This is probably because those who try to prove that there is no God usually take their stand on reason, while those who try to prove the reverse generally take their stand on faith. Such arguments, however, are more often based on prejudice than either reason or faith. They're not about finding Truth but defending and confirming preconceived opinions.

Reason is concerned not with ephemeral opinions but with the established truth of things. Those who possess the faculty of reason in its clarity are never enslaved by prejudice or preconceived opinions. They will neither attempt to prove nor disprove, but after balancing extremes and bringing together all apparent contradictions, they will carefully and dispassionately compare and consider them, and so arrive at Truth.

Reason represents all that is high and noble in us. It distinguishes us from brute creatures blindly following their animal inclinations, and we become more brutish the more we disobey the voice of reason and follow our selfish inclinations.

To the undeveloped and uncharitable mind, all words have narrow applications, but as we expand our awareness and broaden our intelligence, words become filled with rich meanings and lead us to deeper understandings. The word "reason" is, in reality, associated with all that is loving, gentle, moderate, and just. Violent people are "unreasonable," the kind and considerate are "reasonable," while the mentally ill have "lost their reason." We can see, then, that the word "reason" is used, often unconsciously, to point toward love and thoughtfulness, gentleness and sanity. It leads to and is intimately connected with these divine qualities and cannot be separated from them, except for purposes of analysis. So let's stop any foolish quarreling about words, and, like reasonable beings, search for principles and practices that bring us unity and peace.

The following definition of "reason" in *Nuttall's Standard Dictionary of the English Language* will help overcome any remaining concerns anyone may have about the word:

> *The cause, ground, principle, or motive of anything said or done;*
> *efficient cause; final cause; the faculty of intelligence in man;*
> *specially the faculty by which we arrive at necessary truth.*[3]

We see then that "reason" is a term that can almost embrace Truth itself!

This idea is further supported when we look at other languages. Archbishop Richard Chenevix Trench, in his celebrated work *On the Authorized Version of the New Testament*, wrote that the terms "reason" and "word" "are indeed so essentially one and the same that the Greek language has one word for them both" (*logos*).[4] If, to the Greeks, word is reason, then the opening line of John's Gospel in the New Testament (which was originally written in Greek) is actually best translated as "In the beginning was Reason." Taking the concept further, given that one of the definitions of Tao in Lao Tzu's *Tao Te Ching* is reason, then the Chinese translation of John's Gospel runs "In the beginning was the Tao." And the usual translation of Tao as "the Way" leads us to say that the Way is Reason!

Using the divine faculty of reason, we will never be led astray, nor will we follow blind guides. We will, instead, be faithfully adhering to the guidance of the apostle Paul that we "prove all things, and hold fast that which is good" (1 Thessalonians 5:21), for they who follow the light of reason find the Light of Truth.

Essential Points

- Developing the divine faculty of reason brings calm and mental poise, helping us to cheerfully meet the problems and difficulties of life.
- It's true that reason may be enlisted in the service of the lower, self-seeking nature, but a fuller development of reason leads away from the small self and ultimately allies us with the highest, the divine.
- Those who use reason fully are never enslaved by prejudice or pre-conceived opinions. Instead, after balancing extremes and bringing together all apparent contradictions, they will carefully and dispassionately compare and consider them, and so arrive at Truth.
- The word "reason" is, in reality, associated with all that is loving and gentle, moderate, and just, and is the torch that brings us out of the darkness of ignorance and into the Light of Truth.

15

SELF-DISCIPLINE: MANAGING OUR THOUGHTS AND FEELINGS

W e don't really live until we begin to manage our thoughts and feelings; we merely exist. Those who gratify their desires like animals and pursue their inclinations wherever they may lead are happy in the way that beasts can be happy, because they don't know what they're missing. They suffer as beasts suffer because they don't know the way out of suffering. They don't reflect intelligently on their lives, living instead in a series of sensations, longings, and confused memories without any central idea or principle.

The only difference between the life of beasts and that of undisciplined people is the wider variety of desires and greater intensity of suffering that people experience. It may also be said of such people that their souls are dead, being truly dead to all the nobler qualities that constitute life. Not fixing their attention on these qualities, they become lifeless shells bobbing on the ocean of circumstance.

People whose inner lives are ungoverned and chaotic manifest their confusion in the visible conditions of their outer lives in the world. Although for a time, running with the stream of their desires, they may draw to themselves a more or less large share of the outer necessities and comforts of life, they will never achieve any real success nor accomplish any real good. Sooner or later, worldly failure and disaster must follow—the direct result of their failure to properly adjust and regulate the mental forces that make the outer life.

But in the higher consciousness of each person, a saint lies waiting, ready for a resurrection that shall waken us to the realities of existence. With the practice of self-discipline, we rise above the confusion and adjust our conduct to that steadfast center within ourselves. We cease to follow where inclination leads, slow down the runaway expansion of our desires, and live by the dictates of reason and wisdom. Practicing the craft of discipline, we experience greater goodness and wisdom. Where life once held no purpose or meaning, with this kind of self-discipline we begin to consciously mold our own destinies; we are finally "clothed and in our right mind" (Mark 5:15).

So before we can accomplish anything enduring in the world, we must first begin to manage our own minds. This is as true as "two plus two equals four," for "out of the heart spring all the issues of life" (Proverbs 4:23). If we can't govern the forces within ourselves, we can't manage the outer activities that form our visible lives. On the other hand, as we succeed in governing ourselves, we rise to higher and higher levels of power, usefulness, and success in the world.

Three Steps to Self-Discipline

In the process of mastering self-discipline, there are three stages:

1. Control
2. Clarification
3. Renunciation

Control

Discipline is simply controlling the cravings and compulsions for self-gratification that have been controlling us. We resist temptation and guard ourselves against all those selfish gratification tendencies that are so easy and natural and have been dominating us.

Our first step is to manage our appetite. We begin to consume as reasonable and responsible beings, practicing moderation and thoughtfulness in the selection of our food. Our goal is to make our bodies clear instruments through which we may live and act as decent human beings, no longer degrading ourselves by overindulging. We limit our tongues, then our tempers, and, ultimately, every animal desire and tendency.

In the heart of every man and woman is our true, or sacred, Self. This Self may be thought of as an energetic center without which the person we've believed ourselves to be could not exist. Ignoring this Self leads to suffering and confusion. It operates as an ideal of unselfishness and spotless purity at the core of our being. It's our eternal refuge from all the conflicting elements of our small self. It's the rock in the storm, the prophet within, the divine and immortal essence inside us all.

To control our selves is simply to compare all our words and actions to this ideal in the sacred recesses of our hearts and then manage our conduct accordingly. We start living from the inside out instead of outside in.

Clarification

As we practice self-control and get closer and closer to attaining the ideal at this inner center, we are less and less swayed by the compulsions and cravings that lead to grief, pleasure, and pain, and begin to live a different kind of life, based in strength and fortitude.

Control, however, is just the first stage in self-discipline and is immediately followed by a process of clarification. The life we seek requires more than simply restraining any compulsions and cravings that rise within us. We can never arrive at peace or actualize our ideals by merely controlling them; we must release them from our being. Just as a filter clarifies the solids from coffee or butter, we proceed to take self-justifications and other compulsions out of the heart and mind altogether.

It's in this clarifying of the heart and mind that we become strong and godlike, holding firmly to the ideal center within and rendering all temptations powerless and ineffectual. We do this by thoughtful consideration, earnest meditation, and holy aspiration—and as success is achieved, confusion of mind and life pass away, and a calm mind and noble conduct must follow.

True strength, power, and effectiveness emerge through this self-clarification process, for small-self energy is transmuted into higher intellectual and spiritual energy. The life lived in clear thought and deed is a life filled with boundless energy; the toxic life has little energy.

Those who are clear are more able to succeed in their plans and accomplish their purposes than the confused. Where the confused fail, those who have clarified their mind step in and are victorious, because they direct their energies with a calmer mind and greater clarity and strength of purpose.

As we grow in clarity, all the elements that make up a strong and virtuous life are developed with increasing power. As we bring our small selves into alignment and make our passions work for us, we mold the outer circumstances of our lives and influence others for good.

Renunciation

The third stage of self-discipline is renunciation, a process of letting the lower desires and all toxic and unworthy thoughts drop out of the mind and leaving them to perish by refusing to give them any attention. As we bring clarity to mind, we realize that all that appears to be harmful—all apparent darkness—is powerless unless it receives our encouragement, so we can easily ignore it and let it pass out of our lives.

In pursuing this final stage of self-discipline, we then enter into and realize the divine life. We begin to manifest the distinctly divine qualities, such as wisdom, patience, nonresistance, compassion, and love. At this stage, we also become consciously immortal, rising above all the fluctuations and uncertainties of life and living in an intelligent and unchangeable peace.

Effects of Self-Discipline

With discipline, we live; without discipline, we perish. Without self-discipline, we drift lower and lower, until at last we grovel like lost creatures in the mires of our own filth. But with self-discipline, we rise higher and higher, until at last we stand erect in our divine dignity as completed souls, glorified by the radiance of our clarity.

In fact, through this three-step process of self-discipline (control, clarification, and renunciation), we can reach every degree of holiness we set for ourselves. We can even begin to realize our oneness with the central heart of all things—the Creative Source. As a tree grows in beauty, health, and fruitfulness by being carefully pruned and tended, we grow in grace and beauty by cutting away from our minds all thoughts and ideas that lead to harm and by constant and unfailing cultivation of the good.

Some people shrink from self-discipline because it seems painful and repellent in its early stages, while yielding to desire seems sweet and inviting. But the end of such yielding is darkness and unrest, whereas the fruits of self-discipline are immortality and peace.

Essential Points

- People whose inner lives are ungoverned and chaotic must manifest their confusion in the visible conditions of their outer lives.
- If we can't govern the forces within ourselves, we can't manage the outer activities that form our visible lives. On the other hand, as we succeed in governing ourselves, we rise to higher and higher levels of power, usefulness, and success in the world.
- There are three stages in the process of mastering self-discipline: Control, Clarification, and Renunciation.
- Self-discipline is simply controlling the cravings and compulsions that have been controlling us.
- We can never arrive at peace or actualize our ideals by merely controlling them, so in the second step, we clarify our thoughts and release unwanted ideas from our normal habits of thought.
- The third stage of self-discipline is renunciation, a process of letting all toxic and unworthy thoughts drop out of the mind and leaving them to perish by refusing to give them any attention.
- Through this three-step process of self-discipline (control, clarification, and renunciation), we can begin to realize our oneness with the central heart of all things: the Creative Source.

16

THE POWER OF RESOLUTION

Resolution is the force directing and driving all individual progress. Only when we bring resolution to bear in our lives do we consciously and rapidly develop, for a life without resolution is a life without aims, and a life without aims is drifting and unstable. Without resolution, no substantial work can be accomplished, but if you are true to your resolution, you will succeed in accomplishing your purpose.

When we make a resolution, it's usually because we're unhappy with our conditions and are ready to take the first step toward effective management of the mental materials that compose our characters and lives.

Resolution may, of course, be applied to lower, selfish tendencies, but it's usually the companion of noble aims and lofty ideals. The vows of the saintly are holy resolutions to accomplish some victory over the small self, and the beautiful achievements of holy men and women, along with the glorious conquests of the great spiritual teachers, were the result of unswerving resolution.

Resolution lets us tread a higher and greater path than ever before. And though the difficulties to be surmounted may seem great, the golden halo of success illuminates all the dark places along the path.

Resolution is a commitment that is described well by a quote that's usually attributed to Johann von Goethe (but was actually written by

William H. Murray in his journal of a Himalayan expedition), reminding us that

The moment one definitely commits oneself,
then Providence moves too.
All sorts of things occur to help one that would
never otherwise have occurred. [1]

True resolution is the culmination of long thought, extended struggle, or enthusiastic but unsatisfied aspiration. It's no light thing, no whimsical impulse or vague desire, but a solemn and irrevocable determination not to rest nor cease from endeavor until the high purpose that has been declared is fully accomplished.

Half-hearted and premature resolution is no resolution at all,
and is shattered at the first difficulty.

For these reasons, it serves us to take our time in forming a resolution. We should examine our positions carefully, take into consideration every circumstance and difficulty connected with our decisions, and be fully prepared to meet them. We want to be sure that we completely understand the nature of the resolution, that our minds are finally made up, and that we are without fear and doubt on the subject. With the mind so prepared, the resolution that is formed will be sustained, and by the aid of it we will, in due time, accomplish our intended purpose.

Hasty resolutions are futile.
The mind must be fortified to endure.

Dealing with Tribulation

As soon as the resolution to walk a higher path is made, temptation and trials begin. Many people find that no sooner have they decided to lead a truer and nobler life than they are immediately overwhelmed with such a torrent of new temptations and difficulties that their positions are almost unendurable. Because of this, many relinquish their resolution immediately.

But these temptations and trials are a necessary part of the regeneration we seek. In fact, they're our friends; they show us what we're ready to release. For what is the real nature of a resolution? If we think about it, we can see that each resolution we make is the sudden abandonment of a familiar stream of conduct to open up an entirely new channel. And doesn't that mean that what's been normal can't continue anymore?

Think of engineers turning the course of a powerful river in another direction. They must first cut a new channel and take every precaution to avoid failure in the undertaking. But when they come to actually directing the water into its new channel, this flowing force, which has steadily pursued its accustomed course for ages, will become disobedient, and all the patience, care, and skill of the engineers will be required for the successful completion of the work.

The same is true when we determine to turn our course of conduct to higher directions. Having prepared our minds and laid the plans to cut a new channel of thought, we then proceed to redirect our mental forces, which have flowed uninterrupted in one direction so far, into their new course. Immediately after this redirection, their energy will begin to assert itself in the form of the most powerful temptations and trials yet encountered. And this is exactly as it should be; it is the law. So we must hold to our resolution with courage if it's to do its work.

No one can improve on the established law of things, of course, but we can learn to understand it instead of complaining and wishing things were different. Those who understand all that is involved in the regeneration of the mind will "glory in tribulations" (Romans 5:3), knowing that, like the temptations described in chapter 4, only by passing through them can we gain strength, obtain clarity of heart, and arrive at peace.

Just as the engineers finally succeed in getting the river to flow on peacefully in the broader and better channel (perhaps after many mistakes and failures), and as the turbulence of the water is spent and all the dams are removed, so those with resolution in their hearts at last succeed in directing their thoughts and acts into the better and nobler ways to which they aspire. The temptations and trials give place to steadfast strength and settled peace.

If your life is out of harmony with your conscience or if you're anxious to improve your mind and conduct, take the following steps:

1. First, develop your purpose through earnest self-examination and thought, and having arrived at a final conclusion;
2. Frame your resolution, and having done so;
3. Stay the course under all circumstances.

In so doing, you cannot fail to achieve your purpose, for the Great Law always shields and protects those who have resolved deep within their hearts to live a better life, no matter how great and many their failures and mistakes may have been.

Essential Points

- Resolution is the force directing and driving all individual progress. If you are true to your resolution, you will succeed in accomplishing your purpose.
- True resolution is the culmination of long thought, extended struggle, or enthusiastic but unsatisfied aspiration. It's no light thing, no whimsical impulse or vague desire.
- As soon as the resolution to walk a higher path is made, temptation and trials begin, but we must hold to our resolution with courage if it's to do its work.
- Those who understand how we progress know that only by passing through tribulations can we gain strength, obtain clarity of heart, and arrive at peace.
- You cannot fail to achieve your purpose, for the Great Law always shields and protects those who have resolved deep within their hearts to live a better life, no matter how great and many their failures and mistakes may have been.

17

THE ONLY
GLORIOUS CONQUEST

B ecause the way of Truth is barred by the small egoic self, Truth can only be experienced by the conquest of that self. And since the only enemies that can actually hinder us on that way are our own self-justifications, compulsions, and delusions on which they're based, the glory of blessedness can only be arrived at by overcoming our lower natures. This is what the Muslim concept of *jihad* is all about—and only this, really. It's the "way of the peaceful warrior."

Until we realize the necessity of overcoming the delusions of the small self and start cleansing our hearts, we have not found the path that leads to knowledge and peace. Until the small self is transcended, Truth remains unknown. This is the Divine Law, for we cannot keep our delusions and have Truth as well. Error is not dissolved until selfishness is dead.

This overcoming of the small self is no mystical theory but a very real and practical thing. It's a process that must be pursued daily and hourly, with unswerving faith and courageous resolution if any measure of success is to be achieved. Just as fruit can only be produced by carefully and patiently training the tree, the clear and satisfying fruits of holiness can only be obtained by faithfully and patiently training the mind in the growth of right thought and conduct.

Five Steps to Freedom

The process, therefore, follows sequential stages, like the growth of a tree. These five steps, taken together, will let you overcome all bad habits and particular forms of wrongdoing:

1. Suppression
2. Endurance
3. Elimination
4. Understanding
5. Victory

When people fail to overcome their bad habits, it's because they begin at the wrong end. They want to get to the stage of Victory without passing through the previous four stages. They're like orchard keepers who wish for good fruit without training the branches and attending to their trees.

Suppression

Suppression consists of stopping outbursts of temper, hasty or unkind words, selfish indulgences, and so forth, before they take actual form. This is equivalent to the gardener nipping off the useless buds and branches from the tree. It seems a painful process but a necessary one. The tree bleeds while undergoing the process, and the pruner knows that the tree must not be taxed too severely.

This form of suppression is the process of "mortifying the members" of which the apostle Paul speaks (Colossians 3:5). It's the process of purification by nonrepetition described in various Buddhist texts— and it is rarely easy. Just as the tree bleeds when its branch is cut, the heart bleeds when a familiar pattern or habit is suppressed. But like the pruner, we must be gentle with ourselves. We must take one behavior at a time and give ourselves credit when our past patterns have been successfully suppressed.

This suppression is only the beginning of self-conquest, however. As an end itself, with no object of finally purifying the heart, it's a kind of hypocrisy, a hiding of one's true nature, and striving to appear better in the eyes of others than one really is. In that case, it's a harmful practice that hurts more than it helps. But when adopted as the first stage toward complete clarification, it is good, demonstrating forbearance to one's community, helping to refine the character, and leading to the second stage, Endurance.

Endurance

Endurance, or patient self-restraint, is the process of silently weathering the pain we feel when we experience certain actions and attitudes of other minds toward us. As we succeed at this stage, we come to see that all pain and suffering actually arises in our own mind. They're a function of our own bad habits and shortcomings, not the wrong attitudes of others toward us—those are merely the means by which our own bad habits and shortcomings are shown to us.

So, gradually, we release all others from blame for our distress. We can only accuse ourselves, and so we learn to love those who thus unconsciously reveal to us our own bad habits and shortcomings.

Elimination

Having passed through Suppression and Endurance, we enter the third stage, Elimination. Here the unwanted thought that lies behind the unwanted act is cast from the mind as soon as it appears. We realize that the ideas, beliefs, and assumptions we've used are the source of our distress, and we choose to release them from our memories and our daily thoughts. As we do so, conscious strength and spiritual joy begin to take the place of pain and suffering.

Understanding

Then, finally, when the mind has become comparatively calm, we gain deeper insight into its complexities. We begin to understand the onset, growth, and outworking of all our actions, helpful and harmful. This is the stage of Understanding.

Victory

Perfection in understanding leads to the final overcoming of the small self. This is a conquest so complete that harmful habits can no more rise in the mind, even as a thought or impression. For when the knowledge of that habit is complete, when it's known in its totality, from its inception as a seed in the mind to its ripened outgrowth as act and consequence, then it no longer has a place in life but is abandoned forever. Then the mind is at peace. The acts of others no longer arouse wrong and pain in the mind. We become glad, calm, and wise, filled with love and blessedness. And this is Victory!

Essential Points

- There are five steps in the process of overcoming all bad habits: Suppression, Endurance, Elimination, Understanding, and Victory.
- Suppression consists of stopping actions like having outbursts of temper, saying hasty or unkind words, giving in to selfish indulgences, and so forth, before they take actual form.
- Endurance, or patient self-restraint, is the process of silently weathering the pain we feel when we experience certain actions and attitudes of other minds toward us; those are merely the means by which our own bad habits and shortcomings are shown to us.
- Elimination is the stage when the unwanted thought that lies behind the unwanted act is cast from the mind as soon as it appears.
- When the mind has become comparatively calm, we're able to understand its complexities.
- Perfection in understanding leads to the final overcoming of the small self. This is a conquest so complete that harmful habits can no more rise in the mind, even as a thought or impression.

18

CONTENTMENT IN ACTION

To be content doesn't mean there's no more activity or endeavor; it means that our endeavor is free from anxiety. It does not mean being satisfied with selfishness, ignorance, or folly but resting happily in duty done and in goals accomplished, and being peacefully energized by all that's been achieved.

Some may seem to be content to grovel through life suffering and in debt, but this is more like indifference or apathy. To be indifferent to their due responsibilities, obligations, and the just claims of others isn't really contentment. These people don't experience the clear and lasting joy that accompanies active contentment. They're sleeping souls who sooner or later will be awakened by some form of intense suffering. They may suffer great loss or be diagnosed with some frightful disease, but then, having passed through that distress, they'll find that true contentment is the outcome of honest endeavor and achievement.

Misunderstandings

The confusion of a positive spiritual virtue or principle with a negative animal vice is common among thinkers and writers, even in advanced schools of thought. Sadly, a lot of valuable energy has been wasted in criticizing and condemning others' ideas where a little calm reasoning would reveal a greater light and lead to clarity.

For example, the other day, I came across a vigorous attack on the teaching of "love." The writer condemned this kind of teaching as weak, foolish, and hypocritical. Needless to say, what he was condemning as "love" was merely weak sentimentality and hypocrisy.

Another writer, condemning "meekness," doesn't realize that what he calls meekness is only cowardice. Yet another who attacks "chastity" as a "snare" is really confusing painful and hypocritical restraint with the divinely beautiful virtue of chastity. And just recently I received a long letter from a correspondent who took great pains to show me that "contentment" is a vice and thus the source of immeasurable harm.

What my correspondent called "contentment" is actually indifference. And the spirit of indifference is incompatible with progress, whereas the spirit of contentment goes along with the highest form of activity, the truest advancement and development. Apathy is the twin sister of indifference, but cheerful and ready action is the friend of contentment.

There are three things to be content with:

1. *Whatever happens.* Content with whatever happens, we escape grief.
2. *Friends and family.* Content with our friends and family, we avoid anxiety and misery.
3. *Loving thoughts.* Content with loving thoughts, we never go back to suffer and grovel in faults.

With this in mind, there are three things to *not* be content with:

1. *Opinions.* Not content with our opinions, we continually increase in intelligence.
2. *Our character.* Not content with our character, we ceaselessly grow in strength and virtue.
3. *Our spiritual condition.* Not content with our spiritual condition, we enter into greater wisdom and fuller blessedness.

In a word, we should be content with our lives but not indifferent to our development as responsible and spiritual beings.

Truly contented people work energetically and faithfully, and they accept all results with an untroubled, trusting spirit. With the growth of understanding, they know which results exactly correspond with what endeavors. Whatever material possessions come to them will come not by greed, anxiety, or strife but by their own noble thought, wise action, and effortless endeavor.

Essential Points

• To be contented means that our endeavors are free from anxiety; we are resting happily in duty done and in goals accomplished and are peacefully energized by all that's been achieved.

• Cheerful and ready action is the friend of contentment, while apathy is the twin of indifference.

• Contented with whatever happens, we escape grief; contented with our friends and family, we avoid anxiety and wretchedness; contented with loving thoughts, we never suffer and grovel in faults.

• Not content with our opinions, we will continually increase in intelligence; not content with our character, we will ceaselessly grow in strength and virtue; and not content with our spiritual condition, we will enter into greater wisdom and fuller blessedness.

19

THE TEMPLE OF ONENESS

Universal Oneness is the supreme ideal of humanity, and the world is slowly but steadily moving toward that ideal. Today, as never before, great numbers of people all over the world are striving to make this ideal tangible and real. With the aid of the internet and satellite communications, no one is isolated in this endeavor, and all are supported by someone somewhere.

The unselfish elements in all such endeavors can't fail to have their effect on humanity and are certainly urging us toward achieving our noblest aspirations. But sadly the ideal state has not yet manifested, and societies formed to encourage Oneness are continually being shattered to pieces by internal dissension.

This is because the purely spiritual nature of Oneness is not perceived; the principles involved, as well as the individual behaviors necessary to experience it, are not understood. The Oneness humanity seeks is withheld from our experience by humanity itself, its progress often hindered by those who desire and work zealously for it.

It comes down to this: Oneness can't be experienced by humanity as long as any degree of self-seeking reigns in the hearts of men and women around the world, for self-seeking tears apart the seamless coat of loving unity.

Nonetheless, any individual may realize Oneness in its perfection and know it in all its beauty and completion. If anyone will consciously become a wise, clear, and loving spirit, remove from the mind every element of strife, and learn to practice the divine qualities, Oneness will be their experience and no longer a mere theory, opinion, or illusive dream.

This is because Oneness begins as an inner spiritual experience, and its external manifestation in the world must evolve via a natural sequence. As a spiritual reality, it must be discovered by each person for himself or herself in the only place where spiritual realities can be found—within oneself. And it rests with each whether to choose it or to refuse it.

Obstacles to Oneness

There are four tendencies in the human mind that destroy Oneness and block its understanding:

1. Pride
2. Self-service
3. Hostility
4. Condemnation

Where these are there can be no Oneness. In whatever heart these hold sway, discord rules and Oneness is not realized, for these tendencies are, in their very nature, dark and selfish and always manifest as disruption and destruction. From these four tendencies proceeds that serpent brood of false actions and conditions that poison people's hearts and fill the world with suffering and sorrow.

Pride

Out of the habit of pride proceed envy, resentment, and bullheadedness. Pride includes envy of the position, influence, and goodness of others. Prideful people think, *I am more deserving than this man or this woman.* They also continually find occasion for resenting the actions of

others, saying, "I have been snubbed" and "I have been insulted."
Thinking only of their own excellence, the prideful see no excellence
in others.

Self-Service

From self-serving habits proceed egotism, lust for power, belittling, and
contempt. Self-service worships the personality in which it moves; it's
lost in the adoration and glorification of that "I," the self that has no
real existence but is a dark dream and a delusion. It desires preeminence
over others and thinks, "I am great," and "I am more important than
others." It also belittles others, and bestows contempt upon them,
seeing no beauty in them. The egoic small self, the personality, is lost in
the consideration of its own beauty.

In the darkness of these self-serving tendencies, people believe that
they can fight wars to ensure peace, kill to save lives, end injury by
injuring, restore love by hating, find unity through contention, create
kindness with cruelty, and establish Oneness by erecting their own
opinions (which in time they themselves will abandon as worthless) as
objects of universal adoration.

Hostility

From hostile thoughts proceed slander, cruelty, revilement, and anger.
Hostility strives to overcome harm by adding harm to it. It says, "This
person has spoken ill of me; I'll speak poorly of him to teach him a
lesson." It mistakes cruelty for kindness and causes its possessor to
revile a reproving friend. It feeds the flames of anger with bitter and
rebellious thoughts.

Condemnation

From condemning thoughts proceed accusation, false pity, and false
judgment. Condemnation feeds itself on the contemplation of harm,
and cannot see the good. It has eyes for only the harmful and finds it in
almost every person, thing, and idea. It sets up an arbitrary standard of
right and wrong for judging others and thinks, "This person doesn't do

as I would have her do; she is therefore evil, and I will denounce her." So blind is condemnation that while rendering its possessors incapable of judging themselves, it causes them to set themselves up as the judges of all things.

• • •

From these four tendencies—pride, self-service, hostility, condemnation—no element of Oneness can proceed. They are deadly mental poisons, and those who allow them to fester cannot experience the peaceful principles on which Oneness rests.

Qualities Encouraging Oneness

Four divine qualities lead to the experience of Oneness and they are, in a way, the foundation stones on which it rests.

1. Humility
2. Self-surrender
3. Love
4. Compassion

Whenever and wherever these exist, Oneness is active. In whatever heart these qualities are dominant, Oneness is an established reality. For these four divine qualities are, in their very nature, filled with the revealing Light of Truth. There is no darkness in them and where they are, their light is so powerful that no dark tendencies can remain; darkness dissolves and dissipates. Out of these four qualities proceed all those angelic actions and conditions that make for unity and bring gladness to the heart of humanity and to the world.

1. From the spirit of humility proceed contentment and peace;
2. From self-surrender come patience, wisdom, and true judgment;
3. From love spring kindness, joy, and harmony; and
4. From compassion proceed gentleness and forgiveness.

Those who bring themselves into harmony with these four qualities are divinely enlightened. They can see the source of people's actions and where they're headed. Therefore, they can no longer exercise the darker tendencies described above.

Oneness is freedom from any tendency toward malice, envy, bitterness, contention, or condemnation. Where two are determined to maintain an opposing opinion, clinging to self and ill will, Oneness is absent. Where two are prepared to sympathize with each other, to see no evil in each other, to serve and not attack each other, the Love of Truth and goodwill are there and Oneness is present.

In Truth we are all One—those who live blindly as well as those who are enlightened—and when those who grope in the darkness are able finally perceive the glory and beauty of the Light of Truth, the darkness will be dispelled from their minds and they, too, will experience the One. They'll know the effective attitude of mind toward all: goodwill.

Of the four dark tendencies are born ill will and strife;
Of the four divine qualities are born goodwill and peace.
Living in the four dark tendencies makes us strife producers.
Living in the four divine qualities makes us peacemakers.

The theories and schemes for propagating Oneness are many, but Oneness itself is unchangeable. It consists of erasing all egotism and strife and practicing goodwill and peace, for Oneness is a practice, not a theory. Self-surrender and goodwill are its guardian angels, and peace is its dwelling place.

The wished-for Temple of Oneness will be erected in the world when its four foundation stones of *humility, self-surrender, love,* and *compassion* are firmly laid in the hearts of all, for Oneness consists, first and foremost, in the individual's dissolving of the small self. All strife, division, and war are products of the proud, unyielding, egoic self; all peace, unity, and concord are the result of yielding up that small self. Oneness is only practiced and known by those whose hearts are at peace with themselves and the whole world.

Essential Points

- Universal Oneness is the supreme ideal of humanity, and the world is slowly but steadily moving toward that ideal.
- The Oneness humanity seeks is withheld from our experience by humanity itself because the purely spiritual nature of Oneness is not perceived and the principles and behaviors necessary to experience it are not understood.
- The four chief tendencies in the human mind that destroy Oneness and block its understanding are pride, self-service, hostility, and condemnation.
- The four divine qualities that lead to the experience of Oneness are Humility, Self-surrender, Love, and Compassion.
- Oneness itself is unchangeable. It consists of ceasing all egotism and strife and practicing goodwill and peace, for Oneness is a practice, not a theory.

20

UNDOING PREJUDICE, DISCOVERING PEACE

Those who hope to better themselves and humanity constantly aim for an attitude of mind that is a blessing to themselves and others. To accomplish this, we put ourselves mentally and sympathetically in the place of others, learning about their experience, understanding their particular frame of mind, and feeling for them instead of harshly and falsely judging them, since judging others makes us unhappy and takes away their happiness as well.

One of the great obstacles to the attainment of such an attitude of mind is prejudice, and until that's removed, it's impossible for us to act toward others as we wish others to act toward us. As long as people are determined to cling to their preconceived opinions, mistaking them for Truth and refusing to consider dispassionately the positions of others, they can neither escape hostility nor arrive at blessedness.

Prejudice destroys kindness, sympathy, love, and true judgment. The strength of someone's prejudices determines their harshness and unkindness toward others, for prejudice and cruelty are inseparable.

This is because there's no reasoning in prejudice. It's immediately aroused and then people no longer act reasonably, giving way to rashness, anger, or violence. They don't consider their words nor do they regard the feelings and rights of others. They have, for the time being, forfeited their humanity and have descended below the level of an irrational creature.

Those who strive for gentleness and aim to act unselfishly toward others will put away all their delusional prejudices and petty opinions. In doing so, they'll gradually acquire the power of thinking and feeling for others—of understanding their particular state of knowledge. They will, in time, enter fully into the others' hearts and lives, sympathizing with them and seeing them as they are.

People who make this effort don't oppose the prejudices of others by introducing their own but seek instead to undo prejudice by introducing sympathy and love into the situation. They'll strive to bring out all that's good in others, encouraging the good by appealing to it and discouraging the harm by ignoring it. Moreover, they'll realize the good in the all the unselfish endeavors of others, though their methods may be very different from their own, and will thus rid their hearts of hostility and fill them instead with love and blessedness.

Those who are prone to harshly judge and condemn others would benefit from asking how far they themselves fall short. They might also remember their own suffering when they were misjudged and misunderstood. Then, gathering wisdom and love from their own bitter experiences, they can studiously avoid piercing those hearts that are still too weak to ignore the thrust and still too immature and uninstructed to understand.

Before condemning others, people need to ask themselves whether they really are better than the people they've singled out as the object of their bitterness. If they are, let them instead feel sympathy for the less-developed souls. If they aren't, let them show reverence for those who've gone beyond them, lifting themselves up to the purer level.

Eradicating the Appearance of Evil

For thousands of years the great spiritual teachers have taught that evil is only overcome by good, yet still most people haven't learned the lesson. It's profound in its simplicity but difficult to learn, because people are blinded by the illusions of the small egoic self. All over the world, people are still resenting, condemning, and fighting what they see as evil in others. In the process, they increase the delusion in their own hearts that evil has any power while they add to the world's sum of misery and suffering. When they find out that their own resentment is all that must be eradicated and then begin to put love in its place, the appearance of evil will dissolve for lack of sustenance.

> *With burning brain and heart of hate,*
> *I sought my wronger, early, late,*
> *And all the wretched night and day*
> *My dream and thought was slay, and slay.*

> *My better self rose uppermost,*
> *The beast within my bosom lost*
> *Itself in love; peace from afar*
> *Shone o'er me radiant like a star.*

> *I slew my wronger with a deed,*
> *A deed of love; I made him bleed*
> *With kindness, I filled for years*
> *His soul with tenderness and tears.*[1]

Dislike, resentment, and condemnation are all forms of hostility, and the appearance of evil will not end until these are taken out of the heart.

But obliterating the idea of injuries from the mind is merely one of the beginnings in wisdom. There's a still higher and better way, and that way is to purify the heart and enlighten the mind so that instead of having to forget injuries, there are none to remember. For only pride and the small self can be injured and wounded by the actions and attitudes of others, and those who take pride and self out of their hearts can never think the thought, *I have been injured by another or I have been wronged by another.*

Those who think, *This person has injured me,* have not perceived the Truth in life; they fall short of enlightenment, spreading about the untrue idea that evil is a thing to be hated and resented. These people are troubled and disturbed about the transgressions of others, but they are far from Truth. Meanwhile, those who are troubled and disturbed about their own bad habits and shortcomings are very near to the Gate of Wisdom. Those in whose hearts the flames of resentment burn cannot know peace nor understand Truth; those who banish resentment from their hearts can know and understand.

With the uplifting of enlightenment, evildoing becomes impossible. Those who have taken the belief in evil out of their hearts cannot resent or resist it in others, for they understand its origin and nature and know it as a manifestation of ignorance. Those who do harm do not understand; those who understand do not act immorally or maliciously, for from a purified heart proceeds an accurate understanding of how things work, and from accurate understanding proceeds a life that is peaceful, freed from bitterness and suffering, calm, and wise.

Blessed are those who have no wrongs to remember, no injuries to forget, and in whose loving hearts no hostile thought about another can take root and flourish. The loving maintain their tenderness of heart toward those who ignorantly imagine they can do them harm. The attitude of others toward them does not trouble them. Their hearts are at rest in compassion and love.

For those who aim at a life built on the ten divine qualities, who believe that they love Truth, let them stop opposing others and let them strive to calmly and wisely understand them. In so acting toward others, they will be conquering their own lesser selves. And while sympathizing with others, their own souls will be fed with the heavenly dews of kindness and their hearts will be strengthened and refreshed in the pleasant pastures of peace.

Essential Points

- One of the great obstacles to the attainment of a blessed attitude of mind is prejudice, and until that's removed it's impossible for us to act toward others as we would wish others to act toward us.

- There's no reasoning in prejudice. It's immediately aroused and then people no longer act reasonably, giving way to rashness, anger, or violence without considering their words or regarding the feelings and rights of the people they're judging.
- Those who are prone to harshly judge and condemn others would benefit from asking how far they themselves fall short, remember their own suffering when they were misjudged and misunderstood, and, gathering wisdom and love from their own bitter experiences, studiously avoid piercing the hearts of those who may have appeared to do them wrong.
- The loving maintain their tenderness of heart toward those who ignorantly imagine they can do them harm.
- For those who aim at a life built on the ten divine qualities, who believe that they love Truth, let them stop opposing others and strive to calmly and wisely understand them, and their hearts will be strengthened and refreshed in the pleasant pastures of peace.

EXERCISES

1

This last section has given us all the tools we need to change our thinking and to transform our lives. Using them consistently practically guarantees a shift from a life of distress to a life of blessedness. However, since it's taken decades for us to become who we are today and to be where we are today, it will take some time to undo the habits of thought that got us here.

So if you wish to transform your life, set aside twenty-eight days to do the following processes. Start a journal specifically for this series of exercises. At the end of the twenty-eight days, you will see significant changes, and if you want more, take a two-week break and start again.

1. Transforming Thought, Transforming Life

A. Consider the following list of thought processes that lead to distress and misery. Write the first one in your journal and see if you can remember the last time you thought, spoke, or acted out of it.

Describe that experience on the line below it. Then skip a line or two and write the next one, repeating the process for all ten.

1. Lust
2. Hostility
3. Greed
4. Self-indulgence
5. Self-seeking
6. Vanity
7. Pride
8. Doubt
9. Beliefs and assumptions based on fear
10. Delusion

B. Now do the same for the ten divine qualities:

1. Clear, undistracted focus
2. Patience
3. Humility
4. Surrender
5. Self-reliance
6. Fearlessness
7. Knowledge
8. Wisdom
9. Compassion
10. Love

C. Now go back and look at the first ten, the distress-causing thoughts, and on the line below your description of the last time you used that thought process, rewrite the experience as if you had used some of the ten divine qualities instead.

D. On the last double-page spread of your journal, make a chart with the ten sorrow-producing thoughts and ten divine qualities along one side and the numbers 1–28 across the top. Draw lines between the numbers, so it will look something like the table on page 137, extending out to the twenty-eighth day and the tenth divine quality:

E. For twenty-eight days, at the end of each day, simply check off whether you've used that thought process that day. If you've used one of the first ten, then go back to the beginning of your journal, put the date at the top of the next blank page, and write the experience as you remember it. Then rewrite it as it might have happened using the divine qualities instead. Imagine in as great detail as possible, using all your senses (What colors were present? What sounds? What tastes and odors? What textures?), how it might have been if you had been creating a blessing instead of misery.

F. When you're done, appreciate the experience as a learning opportunity and imagine the possibilities of a life filled with the blessings you've created in your rewriting of the experience. Then go to bed; the process you've done will rewire your subconscious mind as you sleep to focus on blessings more than sorrow tomorrow.

2. Discovering the Seed Thought and Uprooting It

A. If you're troubled, perplexed, sorrowful, or unhappy, look at the two lists in exercise 1 and, considering the past three weeks, ask yourself:

- "What mental seeds have I been sowing?"
- "Are they seeds of trouble and sorrow or gratitude and love?"
- "What is my attitude toward others?"
- "What have I been for my friends and family and what have I done for them?"
- "Am I reaping joyous fruits from my beliefs, thoughts, and actions toward others, or am I reaping bitter weeds?"

Creating Your Transformation Tracking System

Thought	Day 1	Day 2	Day 3	Day 4	Day 5	Day 6	Day 7	Day 8	Day...
Lust									
Hatred									
Greed									
Self-indulgence									
Self-seeking									
Vanity									
Pride									
Doubt									
Fear beliefs									
Delusion									

B. In your journal, write down the ways you have been sowing seeds of trouble and sorrow over the past three weeks by using the first ten, sorrow-producing thought processes. Note the times and places you used or experienced these processes.

C. Now rewrite those same times and places as if you'd been using the ten divine qualities instead. Again, imagine in as great detail as possible, using all your senses (What colors were present? What sounds? What tastes and odors? What textures?), how it might have been if you had been creating a blessing instead of misery.

D. Look ahead to the next few days and imagine using the ten divine qualities in your planned experiences. Write a description of those upcoming events as if you have already experienced them based on the ten divine qualities. Again, use all your senses. Now describe how it feels to be that way: feel the joy, the ease, the comfort, the freedom and write about it. You may even want to sing or draw or dance about it, and that's great!

E. Now set all this aside and go about your day, returning to your journal and repeating the process the next time you feel uncomfortable with your life.

3. Future Focus

If you're ready to improve your mind, life, and conduct, it's time to set an intention and use the power of Resolution.

A. Put today's date on a blank page in your journal and write down all the ideas you have about what a perfect life might look like. List everything that you think might bring you joy—in the areas of work, relationships, finances, environment, and spiritual development.

B. Do this for several days over a couple of weeks, starting fresh each time. The list will evolve and change, and that's fine. As you do the other exercises in this book, you are changing.

C. After you've done at least five lists, go over them and make up a list that feels like the best combination of all of them. (Feel free to add new things—you're changing!) Compare your new list with the ten divine qualities. Are there things you want to change to bring them into alignment? For example, you may have on your list "A new car," but would "Easy, reliable, comfortable transportation" be more accurate? You may have written "My daughter behaving properly," but would "My relationship with my daughter is loving and fulfilling for both of us" be more aligned with your goals? You may have noted "Having a different boss," but would "All my relationships, including those at work, are harmonious and effective" accomplish a higher end?

D. Now identify one, two, or three actions you can take to bring this list closer to reality. It may be changing jobs or letting go of an addiction. It may be giving yourself time for self-care. It may be giving your family more of your loving attention. It may be working more productively and efficiently. Whatever they are, turn to a new page in your journal and write them down as specifically as possible. Then go back and compare them to the list of ten divine qualities, making any changes to bring them into alignment with Truth and your fullest satisfaction.

E. When you've clarified the possible actions, write one at the top of a new page in your journal. Imagine implementing this action. Use all your senses—sight, hearing, taste, touch, and smell—to imagine the colors, textures, and other dimensions of how it will feel, what your life will be like, and what the people around you will do and say, then write all of this on the page. Pay attention to how your body is reacting to all this and write that down too. Is it excited? Peaceful and calm? Tensing up? Going into symptoms of fear? Joyful? Longing?

F. Do the same for all the possible actions you've come up with.

G. Now look at what you've written and modify the actions so that your body feels good when you imagine them. Then select the one that feels best. In this way you're developing your resolution through earnest thought and self-examination.

H. Having arrived at a final conclusion, frame your resolution. Write a statement in your journal regarding the action in the present tense, using "I." For example, "I care for myself with ease and joy; each day I set aside at least half an hour simply to do what's best for me." Or something like, "My family is my number one priority, after my own spiritual and physical well-being, therefore I spend quality time each day with my spouse and each of my children." Or perhaps, "My work is my self-expression in the universe; I am capable and effective in all that I do and I receive more than adequate financial and emotional compensation." Or maybe, "I am free of all addictions; my life is my own, and I consciously choose every word and every action." The claim you write becomes your resolution. You may want to write it on a card to put in your wallet, use a dry-erase pen to write it on a mirror, or set it up as a screensaver on your computer or cell phone to remind you of this all-important intention.

I. Stay the course under all circumstances. The world will come back with all kinds of opportunities to do things the way "they've always been done." It will ask you "Are you sure?" in several ways over several weeks. But if you've done this work, you know the answer: you're sure that this is what you intend and are resolved that it be so. So stay the course! Hold fast to your new image of your life and yourself. Don't let anyone tell you it's not possible; they're just mirroring your own lingering doubts. Do what you've resolved to do for twenty-eight days and you're home free. Congratulations! If you're ever tempted to fall back into the old ways again, you'll recognize it immediately as what it is and focus on the new driving force in your life: your resolution.

NOTES

Religious Texts

Biblical references in the "Interpretations" section of this book are from the English Standard Version or the New International Version and sometimes the King James Version, depending on which seemed clearer. James Allen's original text did not include citations, because he used what were then well-known quotations from the only English translation available at that time and place: the King James Version.

Note from the Editor

1. Summaries of the research supporting this understanding may be found in G. Frank Lawlis's *Transpersonal Medicine* and in Michael Murphy's *The Future of the Body*. Additional research is ongoing at the Heartmath Institute, the Institute of Noetic Sciences, and the National Institutes of Health. G. Frank Lawlis, *Transpersonal Medicine: The New Approach to Healing Body-Mind-Spirit* (Boston: Shambhala, 1996); Michael Murphy, *The Future of the Body: Explorations into the Further Evolution of Human Nature* (Los Angeles: J. P. Tarcher, 1992).

Introduction

1. Murdo Carruthers, "James Allen: A Prophet of Meditation," *Herald of the Star 5* (March 1916): 141.

2. Ibid.

3. *The Herald of the Golden Age* was the journal of the Order of the Golden Age, an international animal rights society with a religious and theosophical orientation, operating 1896–1959. A full archive of the journal can be found at the Internet Archive, www.archive.org.

4. Carruthers, "James Allen: A Prophet of Meditation," 142.

5. Lily L. Allen, "Editor's Preface," in *Foundation Stones to Happiness and Success*, by James Allen (New York: Thomas Y. Crowell Company, 1913).

6. James Allen, "Comment on Confucius," in *Theosophy in Australia* (June 1, 1909), the James Allen Free Library, http://james-allen .in1woord.nl/other/Comment-on-Confucius;Knowledge.pdf.

7. The epigraph that begins the introduction is an excerpt from James Allen's "The Path to Prosperity" in *From Poverty to Power, or The Realization of Prosperity and Peace* (Libertyville, IL: Sheldon University Press, 1908).

INTERPRETATIONS

As We Think

Chapter 2—The Effect of Thought on Circumstances

1. Johann Wolfgang von Goethe is usually cited as the author of the quote describing this process, but it turns out it is actually from

The Scottish Himalayan Expedition by William Hutchinson Murray (London: J. M. Dent & Co, 1951). It is also outlined in Ralph Waldo Emerson's essay "Spiritual Laws" (1841) and in *Natural Abundance, Ralph Waldo Emerson's Guide to Prosperity*, edited by Ruth L. Miller (Hillsboro, OR: Beyond Words Publishing, 2011).

2. Ella Wheeler Wilcox, "Will," *Poems of Power* (Chicago: W. B. Conkey Company, 1908), 116.

Chapter 6—Visions and Ideals
1. Stanton Davis Kirkham, *Where Dwells the Soul Serene* (San Francisco: P. Elder, 1907), 127.

Light on Life
Introduction—The Light of Wisdom
1. The foreword and three chapters in the modern adaptation *Light on Life*—"The Simple Facts of Life," "As You Think," and "Replacing Slave Mentality with Sage Mentality"—were adapted from "Light on Facts and Hypothesis," the second chapter of the original text, *Light on Life's Difficulties* (1912).

Chapter 2—As You Think
1. In this quote about the cessation of suffering, Allen is referring to the Third Noble Truth of Theravada Buddhism. Gautama, called the Buddha, explained the Four Noble Truths in his very first sermon, and the Four Truths are explained again and again throughout the Buddhist scriptures, with greater detail and in different ways. Walpola Rahula, *What the Buddha Taught* (Bedford, England: G. Fraser, 1959), 514–24.

2. Ralph Waldo Emerson, "Plato; or, The Philosopher," *Representative Men: Seven Lectures* (London: H. G. Bohn, 1850); Matthew 5:48.

To Rise Above

Chapter 1—True Happiness

1. Edwin Arnold, *The Light of Asia* (London: Trübner, 1879), Book XIII.

2. Ralph Waldo Emerson, "Success," in *Society and Solitude: Twelve Chapters* (Boston: Fields, Osgood, 1870), 265–95.

Chapter 3—Overcoming Self

1. Wayne W. Dyer, *Your Sacred Self: Making the Decision to Be Free* (New York: Harper, 1996); H. Emilie Cady, *Lessons in Truth*, Unity Classic Library (Unity Village, MO: Unity Books, 2007); and Ruth L. Miller, *Coming into Freedom: Emilie Cady's Lessons in Truth for the 21st Century* (Portland, OR: WiseWoman Press, 2009).

2. Cady, *Lessons in Truth*, 85–96.

Chapter 4—The Uses of Temptation

1. Foundation for Inner Peace. *A Course in Miracles: Combined Volume*, 2nd ed., (Glen Ellen, CA: Foundation for Inner Peace, 1992).

2. In Sanskrit, *Trishna* means "thirst" (enthusiastic, vigorous, greedy).

3. In Vedic mythology, *Indra* is the thunder god, the undoing aspect of divinity.

4. Edwin Arnold, *The Light of Asia* (London: Trübner, 1879), Book XIII.

Chapter 5—The Soul of Integrity

1. Edwin Arnold, *The Light of Asia* (London: Trübner, 1879), Book XIII.

2. This is the essence of the Prayer of St. Francis: "where there is darkness, let me bring light . . . where there is hatred, love . . ."

Chapter 7—Belief: The Basis of Action

1. This is the essential teaching and practice given in *A Course in Miracles: Combined Volume*, 2nd ed. (Glen Ellen, CA: Foundation for Inner
Peace, 1992).

2. This is the opening line of most translations of the Qur'an. It has a
parallel in Judaism: "Hear O Israel, the Lord your god is One"
(Deuteronomy 6:4).

3. The word *sin* does not exist in Hebrew or Greek. In Latin, *sin* means
"without," but the Greek word used in the New Testament,
peccatoris, is an archery term meaning "missed the mark," and the
Hebrew word *pasha*, used in the Hebrew Bible or Old Testament,
means "off the path," which may be why some translations of the
Lord's Prayer use the term *trespasses*.

Chapter 9—Thought and Action

1. See Mark 4:22, Mark 10:26, Luke 8:17, or Luke 12:2.

2. Brother [Nicholas Herman] Lawrence, *The Practice of the Presence of
God*, trans. Robert J. Edmonson, ed. Hal M. Helms (Brewster, MA:
Paraclete, 2010).

Chapter 11—Sowing and Reaping

1. The weeds are a reference to the parable of the tares in Matthew
13:24–30.

2. Edwin Arnold, *The Light of Asia* (London: Trübner, 1879), Book
XIII.

Chapter 13—The Supreme Justice
1. Edwin Arnold, *The Light of Asia* (London: Trübner, 1879), Book XIII.

Chapter 14—The Use of Reason
1. Alfred Tennyson, *The Holy Grail and Other Poems* (Boston: Fields, Osgood, 1870), 253.

2. Edwin Arnold, *The Light of Asia* (London: Trübner, 1879), Book XIII.

3. Austin P. Nuttall, *Nuttall's Dictionary of the English Language* (New York: Hurst, 1890), 546.

4. Richard Chenevix Trench, *On the Authorized Version of the New Testament* (New York: Redfield, 1858), 51.

Chapter 16—The Power of Resolution
1. Usually attributed to Johann Wolfgang von Goethe, these lines were in fact written by William Hutchinson Murray in *The Scottish Himalayan Expedition* (London: J. M. Dent & Co, 1951).

Chapter 20—Undoing Prejudice, Discovering Peace
1. Robert Loveman, "Revenge," *A Book of Verses* (Philadelphia: J. B. Lippincott, 1900), 59.

Bibliography and Resources

Arnold, Edwin. *The Light of Asia*. London: Trübner, 1879.

Bucke, Richard M. *Cosmic Consciousness: A Study in the Evolution of the Human Mind*. Philadelphia: Innes & Sons, 1901.

Cady, H. Emilie. *Lessons in Truth*. Unity Village, MO: Unity Books, 1995.

Carus, Paul. *The Gospel of Buddha According to Old Records*. Chicago: Open Court, 1895.

Cousins, Norman. *Anatomy of an Illness as Perceived by the Patient*. New York: W. W. Norton & Company, 2005.

Dyer, Wayne W. *Your Sacred Self: Making the Decision to Be Free*. New York: HarperCollins, 1995.

Emerson, Ralph Waldo. "Plato; or, The Philosopher." In *Representative Men: Seven Lectures*. London: H. G. Bohn, 1850.

Emerson, Ralph Waldo. "Success." In *Society and Solitude: Twelve Chapters*. Boston: Fields, Osgood, 1870.

Foundation for Inner Peace. *A Course in Miracles: Combined Volume*, 2nd ed. Glen Ellen, CA: Foundation for Inner Peace, 1992.

Franklin, Benjamin. *The Autobiography of Benjamin Franklin.* New York: Dover, 1996.

Gandhi, Mohandas K. *Autobiography: The Story of My Experiments with Truth.* Translated by Mahadev Desai. New York: Dover, 1983.

Kirkham, Stanton Davis. *Where Dwells the Soul Serene.* San Francisco: P. Elder, 1907.

Lawlis, G. Frank. *Transpersonal Medicine: The New Approach to Healing Body-Mind-Spirit.* Boston: Shambhala, 1996.

Lawrence [Nicholas Herman]. *The Practice of the Presence of God.* Translated by Robert J. Edmonson; edited by Hal M. Helms. Brewster, MA: Paraclete, 2010.

Miller, Ruth L. *Coming into Freedom: Emilie Cady's Lessons in Truth for the 21st Century.* Portland, OR: WiseWoman, 2009.

Murphy, Michael. *The Future of the Body: Explorations into the Further Evolution of Human Nature.* Los Angeles: J. P. Tarcher, 1992.

Myss, Caroline. *Anatomy of the Spirit: The Seven Stages of Power and Healing.* New York: MJF Books, 2011.

Pert, Candace B. *Molecules of Emotion: Why You Feel the Way You Feel.* New York: Scribner, 1997.

Rahula, Walpola. *What the Buddha Taught.* Bedford, England: G. Fraser, 1959.

Tennyson, Alfred. *The Holy Grail and Other Poems.* Boston: Fields, Osgood, 1870.

Trench, Richard Chenevix. *On the Authorized Version of the New Testament.* 6th ed. New York: Redfield, 1858.

Books by James Allen

Above Life's Turmoil (1910)

All These Things Added (1903) (later published as *Entering the Kingdom* and *The Heavenly Life*)

As a Man Thinketh (1902)

Byways to Blessedness (1904)

The Divine Companion, edited by Lily L. Allen (1919)

Eight Pillars of Prosperity (1911)

Foundation Stones to Happiness and Success, edited by Lily L. Allen (1913)

From Passion to Peace (1910)

From Poverty to Power; or, The Realization of Prosperity and Peace (1901) (contains *The Path to Prosperity* and *The Way of Peace*)

James Allen's Book of Meditations for Every Day in the Year, edited by Lily L. Allen (1913)

The Life Triumphant: Mastering the Heart and Mind (1908)

Light on Life's Difficulties (1912)

Man: King of Mind, Body and Circumstance (1911)

The Mastery of Destiny (1909)

Men and Systems, edited by Lily L. Allen (1914)

Morning and Evening Thoughts (1909)

Out from the Heart (1904)

Poems of Peace (includes the lyrical-dramatic poem "Eolaus") (1907)

The Shining Gateway, edited by Lily L. Allen (1915)

Through the Gate of Good; or, Christ and Conduct (1903)

Online Sources for James Allen

The James Allen Library: http://www.jamesallenlibrary.com

The James Allen Free Library: http://james-allen.in1woord.nl/

Project Gutenberg: http://www.gutenberg.org

The Internet Archive: http://www.archive.org

ORIGINAL TEXT

AS A MAN THINKETH

As Published in 1903

Mind is the master power that molds and makes,
And we are mind, and evermore we take
The tool of thought, and, shaping what we will,
Bring forth a thousand joys, a thousand ills—
We think in secret, and it comes to pass:
Environment is but our looking-glass.

FOREWORD

This little volume (the result of meditation and experience) is not intended as an exhaustive treatise on the much-written upon subject of the power of thought. It is suggestive rather than explanatory, its object being to stimulate men and women to the discovery and perception of the truth that:

They themselves are makers of themselves

by virtue of the thoughts which they choose and encourage; that mind is the master-weaver, both of the inner garment of character and the outer garment of circumstance, and that, as they may have hitherto woven in ignorance and pain they may now weave in enlightenment and happiness.

James Allen

1

THOUGHT AND CHARACTER

The aphorism, "As a man thinketh in his heart so is he," not only embraces the whole of a man's being, but is so comprehensive as to reach out to every condition and circumstance of his life. A man is literally *what he thinks*, his character being the complete sum of all his thoughts.

As the plant springs from, and could not be without, the seed, so every act of a man springs from the hidden seeds of thought, and could not have appeared without them. This applies equally to those acts called "spontaneous" and "unpremeditated" as to those which are deliberately executed.

Act is the blossom of thought, and joy and suffering are its fruits; thus does a man garner in the sweet and bitter fruitage of his own husbandry.

Thought in the mind hath made us. What we are
By thought we wrought and built. If a man's mind
Hath evil thoughts, pain comes on him as comes
The wheel the ox behind . . .

If one endure
in purity of thought

joy follows him
as his own shadow—sure.

Man is a growth by law, and not a creation by artifice, and cause and effect is as absolute and undeviating in the hidden realm of thought as in the world of visible and material things. A noble and Godlike character is not a thing of favour or chance, but is the natural result of continued effort in right thinking, the effect of long-cherished association with Godlike thoughts. An ignoble and bestial character, by the same process, is the result of the continued harbouring of grovelling thoughts.

Man is made or unmade by himself; in the armoury of thought he forges the weapons by which he destroys himself. He also fashions the tools with which he builds for himself heavenly mansions of joy and strength and peace. By the right choice and true application of thought, man ascends to the Divine Perfection; by the abuse and wrong application of thought, he descends below the level of the beast. Between these two extremes are all the grades of character, and man is their maker and master.

Of all the beautiful truths pertaining to the soul which have been restored and brought to light in this age, none is more gladdening or fruitful of divine promise and confidence than this—that man is the master of thought, the moulder of character, and maker and shaper of condition, environment, and destiny.

As a being of Power, Intelligence, and Love, and the lord of his own thoughts, man holds the key to every situation, and contains within himself that transforming and regenerative agency by which he may make himself what he wills.

Man is always the master, even in his weakest and most abandoned state; but in his weakness and degradation he is the foolish master who misgoverns his "household." When he begins to reflect upon his condition, and to search diligently for the Law upon which his being is established, he then becomes the wise master, directing his energies with intelligence, and fashioning his thoughts to fruitful issues. Such is the *conscious* master, and man can only thus become by discovering *within himself* the laws of thought; which discovery is totally a matter of application, self-analysis, and experience.

Only by much searching and mining are gold and diamonds obtained, and man can find every truth connected with his being if he will dig deep into the mine of his soul. And that he is the maker of his character, the moulder of his life, and the builder of his destiny, he may unerringly prove, if he will watch, control, and alter his thoughts, tracing their effects upon himself, upon others, and upon his life and circumstances; linking cause and effect by patient practice and investigation, and utilizing his every experience, even to the most trivial, everyday occurrence, as a means of obtaining that knowledge of himself which is Understanding, Wisdom, Power. In this direction, as in no other, is the law absolute that "He that seeketh findeth; and to him that knocketh it shall be opened"; for only by patience, practise, and ceaseless importunity can a man enter the Door of the Temple of Knowledge.

2

EFFECT OF THOUGHT
ON CIRCUMSTANCES

M an's mind may be likened to a garden, which may be intelligently cultivated or allowed to run wild; but whether cultivated or neg-lected, it must, and will, *bring forth*. If no useful seeds are put into it, then an abundance of useless weed seeds will *fall* therein, and will con-tinue to produce their kind.

Just as a gardener cultivates his plot, keeping it free from weeds, and growing the flowers and fruits which he requires, so may a man tend the garden of his mind, weeding out all the wrong, useless, and impure thoughts, and cultivating toward perfection the flowers and fruits of right, useful, and pure thoughts. By pursuing this process, a man sooner or later discovers that he is the master-gardener of his soul, the director of his life. He also reveals, within himself, the laws of thought, and understands with ever-increasing accuracy, how the thought forces and mind elements operate in the shaping of his character, circumstances, and destiny.

Thought and character are one, and as character can only manifest and discover itself through environment and circumstance, the outer conditions of a person's life will always be found to be harmoniously related to his inner state. This does not mean that a man's circumstances at any given time are an indication of his entire character, but that those circumstances are so intimately connected with some vital thought element within himself that, for the time being, they are indispensable to his development.

Every man is where he is by the law of his being. The thoughts which he has built into his character have brought him there, and in the arrangement of his life there is no element of chance, but all is the result of a law which cannot err. This is just as true of those who feel "out of harmony" with their surroundings as of those who are contented with them.

As the progressive and evolving being, man is where he is that he may learn that he may grow; and as he learns the spiritual lesson which any circumstance contains for him, it passes away and gives place to other circumstances.

Man is buffeted by circumstances so long as he believes himself to be the creature of outside conditions. But when he realizes that he is a creative power, and that he may command the hidden soil and seeds of his being out of which circumstances grow, he then becomes the rightful master of himself.

That circumstances grow out of thought every man knows who has for any length of time practiced self-control and self-purification, for he will have noticed that the alteration in his circumstances has been in exact ratio with his altered mental condition. So true is this that when a man earnestly applies himself to remedy the defects in his character, and makes swift and marked progress, he passes rapidly through a succession of vicissitudes.

The soul attracts that which it secretly harbours; that which it loves, and also that which it fears; it reaches the height of its cherished aspirations; it falls to the level of its unchastened desires—and circumstances are the means by which the soul receives its own.

Every thought-seed sown or allowed to fall into the mind, and to take root there, produces its own, blossoming sooner or later into act, and bearing its own fruitage of opportunity and circumstance. Good thoughts bear good fruit, bad thoughts bad fruit.

The outer world of circumstance shapes itself to the inner world of thought, and both pleasant and unpleasant external conditions are factors which make for the ultimate good of the individual. As the reaper of his own harvest, man learns both by suffering and bliss.

Following the inmost desires, aspirations, thoughts, by which he allows himself to be dominated, (pursuing the will-o'-the-wisps of impure imaginings or steadfastly walking the highway of strong and high endeavour), a man at last arrives at their fruition and fulfilment in the outer conditions of his life. The laws of growth and adjustment everywhere obtains.

A man does not come to the almshouse or the jail by the tyranny of fate of circumstance, but by the pathway of grovelling thoughts and base desires. Nor does a pure-minded man fall suddenly into crime by stress of any mere external force; the criminal thought had long been secretly fostered in the heart, and the hour of opportunity revealed its gathered power. Circumstance does not make the man; it reveals him to himself. No such conditions can exist as descending into vice and its attendant sufferings apart from vicious inclinations, or ascending into virtue and its pure happiness without the continued cultivation of virtuous aspirations. And man, therefore, as the lord and master of thought, is the maker of himself, the shaper and author of environment. Even at birth the soul comes to its own, and through every step of its earthly pilgrimage it attracts those combinations of conditions which reveal itself, which are the reflections of its own purity and impurity, its strength and weakness.

Men do not attract that which they *want*, but that which they *are*. Their whims, fancies, and ambitions are thwarted at every step, but their inmost thoughts and desires are fed with their own food, be it foul or clean. The "divinity that shapes our ends" is in ourselves; it is our very self. Only himself manacles man: thought and action are the gaolers of Fate—they imprison, being base. They are also the angels of Freedom—they liberate, being noble. Not what he wishes and prays for does a man get, but what he justly earns. His wishes and prayers are only gratified and answered when they harmonize with his thoughts and actions.

In the light of this truth, what, then, is the meaning of "fighting against circumstances"? It means that a man is continually revolting against an *effect* without, while all the time he is nourishing and preserving its *cause* in his heart. That cause may take the form of a conscious vice or an unconscious weakness; but whatever it is, it stubbornly retards the efforts of its possessor, and thus calls aloud for remedy.

Men are anxious to improve their circumstances, but are unwilling to improve themselves. They therefore remain bound. The man who does not shrink from self-crucifixion can never fail to accomplish the object upon which his heart is set. This is as true of earthly as of heavenly things. Even the man whose sole object is to acquire wealth must be prepared to make great personal sacrifices before he can accomplish his object; and how much more so he who would realize a strong and well-poised life?

Here is a man who is wretchedly poor. He is extremely anxious that his surroundings and home comforts should be improved, yet all the time he shirks his work, and considers he is justified in trying to deceive his employer on the ground of the insufficiency of his wages. Such a man does not understand the simplest rudiments of those principles which are the basis of true prosperity, and is not only totally unfitted to rise out of his wretchedness, but is actually attracting to himself a still deeper wretchedness by dwelling in, and acting out, indolent, deceptive, and unmanly thoughts.

Here is a rich man who is the victim of a painful and persistent disease as the result of gluttony. He is willing to give large sums of money to get rid of it, but he will not sacrifice his gluttonous desires. He wants to gratify his taste for rich and unnatural foods and have his health as well. Such a man is totally unfit to have health, because he has not yet learned the first principles of a healthy life.

Here is an employer of labor who adopts crooked measures to avoid paying the regulation wage, and, in the hope of making larger profits, reduces the wages of his workpeople. Such a man is altogether unfitted for prosperity. And when he finds himself bankrupt, both as regards reputation and riches, he blames circumstances, not knowing that he is the sole author of his condition.

I have introduced these three cases merely as illustrative of the truth that man is the causer (though nearly always is unconsciously) of his circumstances. That, while aiming at the good end, he is continually frustrating its accomplishment by encouraging thoughts and desires which cannot possibly harmonize with that end. Such cases could be multiplied and varied almost indefinitely, but this is not necessary, as the reader can, if he so resolves, trace the action of the laws of thought in his own mind and life, and until this is done, mere external facts cannot serve as a ground of reasoning.

Circumstances, however, are so complicated, thought is so deeply rooted, and the conditions of happiness vary so vastly with individuals, that a man's entire soul condition (although it may be known to himself) cannot be judged by another from the external aspect of his life alone. A man may be honest in certain directions, yet suffer privations. A man may be dishonest in certain directions, yet acquire wealth. But the conclusion usually formed that the one man fails *because of his particular honesty*, and that the other prospers *because of his particular dishonesty*, is the result of a superficial judgment, which assumes that the dishonest man is almost totally corrupt, and honest man almost entirely virtuous. In the light of a deeper knowledge and wider experience, such judgment is found to be erroneous. The dishonest man may have some admirable virtues which the other does not possess; and the honest man obnoxious vices which are absent in the other. The honest man reaps the good results of his honest thoughts and acts; he also brings upon himself the sufferings which his vices produce. The dishonest man likewise garners his own suffering and happiness.

It is pleasing to human vanity to believe that one suffers because of one's virtue. But not until a man has extirpated every sickly, bitter, and impure thought from his mind, and washed every sinful stain from his soul, can he be in a position to know and declare that his sufferings are the result of his good, and not of his bad qualities. And on the way to that supreme perfection, he will have found, working in his mind and life, the Great Law which is absolutely just, and which cannot give good for evil, evil for good. Possessed of such knowledge, he will then know, looking back upon his past ignorance and blindness, that his life is, and always was, justly ordered, and that all his past experiences, good and bad, were the equitable outworking of his evolving, yet unevolved self.

Good thoughts and actions can never produce bad results. Bad thoughts and actions can never produce good results. This is but saying that nothing can come from corn but corn, nothing from nettles but nettles. Men understand this law in the natural world, and work with it. But few understand it in the mental and moral world (though its operation there is just as simple and undeviating), and they, therefore, do not cooperate with it.

Suffering is *always* the effect of wrong thought in some direction. It is an indication that the individual is out of harmony with himself, with the Law of his being. The sole and supreme use of suffering is to purify, to burn out all that is useless and impure. Suffering ceases for him who is pure. There could be no object in burning gold after the dross had been removed, and a perfectly pure and enlightened being could not suffer.

The circumstances which a man encounters with suffering are the result of his own mental inharmony. The circumstances which a man encounters with blessedness are the result of his own mental harmony. Blessedness, not material possessions, is the measure of right thought. Wretchedness, not lack of material possessions, is the measure of wrong thought. A man may be cursed and rich; he may be blessed and poor. Blessedness and riches are only joined together when the riches are rightly and wisely used. And the poor man only descends into wretchedness when he regards his lot as a burden unjustly imposed.

Indigence and indulgence are the two extremes of wretchedness. They are both equally unnatural and the result of mental disorder. A man is not rightly conditioned until he is a happy, healthy, and prosperous being; and happiness, health, and prosperity are the result of a harmonious adjustment of the inner with the outer, of the man with his surroundings.

A man only begins to be a man when he ceases to whine and revile, and commences to search for the hidden justice which regulates his life. And as he adapts his mind to that regulating factor, he ceases to accuse others as the cause of his condition, and builds himself up in strong and noble thoughts; ceases to kick against circumstances, but begins to use them as aids to his more rapid progress, and as a means of discovering the hidden powers and possibilities within himself.

Law, not confusion, is the dominating principle in the universe. Justice, not injustice, is the soul and substance of life. And righteousness, not corruption, is the moulding and moving force in the spiritual government of the world. This being so, man has but to right himself to find that the universe is right; and during the process of putting himself right he will find that as he alters his thoughts toward things and other people, things and other people will alter toward him.

The proof of this truth is in every person, and it therefore admits of easy investigation by systematic introspection and self-analysis. Let a man radically alter his thoughts, and he will be astonished at the rapid transformation it will effect in the material conditions of his life. Men imagine that thought can be kept secret, but it cannot; it rapidly crystallizes into habit, and habit solidifies into circumstance. Bestial thoughts crystallize into habits of drunkenness and sensuality, which solidify into circumstances of destitution and disease: impure thoughts of every kind crystallize into enervating and confusing habits, which solidify into distracting and adverse circumstances: thoughts of fear, doubt, and indecision crystallize into weak, unmanly, and irresolute habits, which solidify into circumstances of failure, indigence, and slavish dependence: lazy thoughts crystallize into habits of uncleanliness and dishonesty, which solidify into circumstances of foulness and beggary: hateful and condemnatory thoughts crystallize into habits of accusation and violence, which solidify into circumstances of injury and persecution: selfish thoughts of all kinds crystallize into habits of self-seeking, which solidify into circumstances more or less distressing. On the other hand, beautiful thoughts of all crystallize into habits of grace and kindliness, which solidify into genial and sunny circumstances: pure thoughts crystallize into habits of temperance and self-control, which solidify into circumstances of repose and peace:

thoughts of courage, self-reliance, and decision crystallize into manly habits, which solidify into circumstances of success, plenty, and freedom: energetic thoughts crystallize into habits of cleanliness and industry, which solidify into circumstances of pleasantness: gentle and forgiving thoughts crystallize into habits of gentleness, which solidify into protective and preservative circumstances: loving and unselfish thoughts crystallize into habits of self-forgetfulness for others, which solidify into circumstances of sure and abiding prosperity and true riches.

A particular train of thought persisted in, be it good or bad, cannot fail to produce its results on the character and circumstances. A man cannot *directly* choose his circumstances, but he can choose his thoughts, and so indirectly, yet surely, shape his circumstances.

Nature helps every man to the gratification of the thoughts, which he most encourages, and opportunities are presented which will most speedily bring to the surface both the good and evil thoughts.

Let a man cease from his sinful thoughts, and all the world will soften towards him, and be ready to help him. Let him put away his weakly and sickly thoughts, and lo, opportunities will spring up on every hand to aid his strong resolves. Let him encourage good thoughts, and no hard fate shall bind him down to wretchedness and shame. The world is your kaleidoscope, and the varying combinations of colours which at every succeeding moment it presents to you are the exquis-itely adjusted pictures of your ever-moving thoughts.

> So You will be what you will to be;
> Let failure find its false content
> In that poor word, "environment,"
> But spirit scorns it, and is free.

> It masters time, it conquers space;
> It cowes that boastful trickster, Chance,
> And bids the tyrant Circumstance
> Uncrown, and fill a servant's place.

The human Will, that force unseen,
The offspring of a deathless Soul,
Can hew a way to any goal,
Though walls of granite intervene.

Be not impatient in delay,
But wait as one who understands;
When spirit rises and commands,
The gods are ready to obey.

3

EFFECT OF THOUGHT ON
HEALTH AND THE BODY

The body is the servant of the mind. It obeys the operations of the mind, whether they be deliberately chosen or automatically expressed. At the bidding of unlawful thoughts the body sinks rapidly into disease and decay; at the command of glad and beautiful thoughts it becomes clothed with youthfulness and beauty.

Disease and health, like circumstances, are rooted in thought. Sickly thoughts will express themselves through a sickly body. Thoughts of fear have been known to kill a man as speedily as a bullet, and they are continually killing thousands of people just as surely though less rapidly. The people who live in fear of disease are the people who get it. Anxiety quickly demoralizes the whole body, and lays it open to the entrance of disease; while impure thoughts, even if not physically indulged, will soon shatter the nervous system.

Strong, pure, and happy thoughts build up the body in vigour and grace. The body is a delicate and plastic instrument, which responds readily to the thoughts by which it is impressed, and habits of thought will produce their own effects, good or bad, upon it.

Men will continue to have impure and poisoned blood so long as they propagate unclean thoughts. Out of a clean heart comes a clean life and a clean body. Out of a defiled mind proceeds a defiled life and corrupt body. Thought is the fount of action, life, and manifestation; make the fountain pure, and all will be pure.

Change of diet will not help a man who will not change his thoughts. When a man makes his thoughts pure, he no longer desires impure food.

Clean thoughts make clean habits. The so-called saint who does not wash his body is not a saint. He who has strengthened and purified his thoughts does not need to consider the malevolent microbe.

If you would perfect your body, guard your mind. If you would renew your body, beautify your mind. Thoughts of malice, envy, disappointment, despondency, rob the body of its health and grace. A sour face does not come by chance; it is made by sour thoughts. Wrinkles that mar are drawn by folly, passion, pride.

I know a woman of ninety-six who has the bright, innocent face of a girl. I know a man well under middle age whose face is drawn into inharmonious contours. The one is the result of a sweet and sunny disposition; the other is the outcome of passion and discontent.

As you cannot have a sweet and wholesome abode unless you admit the air and sunshine freely into your rooms, so a strong body and a bright, happy, or serene countenance can only result from the free admittance into the mind of thoughts of joy and goodwill and serenity.

On the faces of the aged there are wrinkles made by sympathy, others by strong and pure thought, others are carved by passion. Who cannot distinguish them? With those who have lived righteously, age is calm, peaceful, and softly mellowed, like the setting sun. I have recently seen a philosopher on his deathbed. He was not old except in years. He died as sweetly and peacefully as he had lived.

There is no physician like cheerful thought for dissipating the ills of the body; there is no comforter to compare with goodwill for dispersing the shadows of grief and sorrow. To live continually in thoughts of ill will, cynicism, suspicion, and envy, is to be confined in a self-made prison-hole. But to think well of all, to be cheerful with all, to patiently learn to find the good in all—such unselfish thoughts are the very portals of heaven; and to dwell day to day in thoughts of peace toward every creature will bring abounding peace to their possessor.

4

THOUGHT AND PURPOSE

Until thought is linked with purpose there is no intelligent accomplishment. With the majority the bark of thought is allowed to "drift" upon the ocean of life. Aimlessness is a vice, and such drifting must not continue for him who would steer clear of catastrophe and destruction.

They who have no central purpose in their life fall an easy prey to worries, fears, troubles, and self-pityings, all of which are indications of weakness, which lead, just as surely as deliberately planned sins (though by a different route), to failure, unhappiness, and loss, for weakness cannot persist in a power evolving universe.

A man should conceive of a legitimate purpose in his heart, and set out to accomplish it. He should make this purpose the centralizing point of his thoughts. It may take the form of a spiritual ideal, or it may be a worldly object, according to his nature at the time being. But whichever it is, he should steadily focus his thought-forces upon the object, which he has set before him. He should make this purpose his supreme duty, and should devote himself to its attainment, not allowing his thoughts to wander away into ephemeral fancies, longings, and imaginings. This is the royal road to self-control and true concentration of thought. Even if he fails again and again to accomplish his purpose (as he necessarily must until weakness is overcome), *the strength of character gained* will be the measure of *his true* success, and this will form a new starting-point for future power and triumph.

Those who are not prepared for the apprehension of a *great* purpose should fix the thoughts upon the faultless performance of their duty, no matter how insignificant their task may appear. Only in this way can the thoughts be gathered and focused, and resolution and energy be developed, which being done, there is nothing which may not be accomplished.

The weakest soul, knowing its own weakness, and believing this truth that strength can only be developed by effort and practice, *will, thus believing, at once begin to exert itself, and adding effort to effort, patience to patience, and strength to strength, will never cease to develop, and will at last grow divinely strong.*

As the physically weak man can make himself strong by careful and patient training, so the man of weak thoughts can make them strong by exercising himself in right thinking.

To put away aimlessness and weakness, and to begin to think with purpose, is to enter the ranks of those strong ones who only recognize failure as one of the pathways to attainment; who make all conditions serve them, and who think strongly, attempt fearlessly, and accomplish masterfully.

Having conceived of his purpose, a man should mentally mark out a *straight* pathway to its achievement, looking neither to the right nor to the left. Doubts and fears should be rigorously excluded; they are disintegrating elements, which break up the straight line of effort, rendering it crooked, ineffectual, useless. Thoughts of doubt and fear never accomplish anything, and never can. They always lead to failure. Purpose, energy, power to do, and all strong thoughts cease when doubt and fear creep in.

The will to do springs from the knowledge that we *can* do. Doubt and fear are the great enemies of knowledge, and he who encourages them, who does not slay them, thwarts himself at every step.

He who has conquered doubt and fear has conquered failure. His every thought is allied with power, and all difficulties are bravely met and wisely overcome. His purposes are seasonably planted, and they bloom and bring forth fruit, which does not fall prematurely to the ground.

Thought allied fearlessly to purpose becomes creative force. He who *knows* this is ready to become something higher and stronger than a mere bundle of wavering thoughts and fluctuating sensations. He who *does* this has become the conscious and intelligent wielder of his mental powers.

5

THE THOUGHT-FACTOR
IN ACHIEVEMENT

All that a man achieves and all that he fails to achieve is the direct result of his own thoughts. In a justly ordered universe, where loss of equipoise would mean total destruction, individual responsibility must be absolute. A man's weakness and strength, purity and impurity, are his own, and not another man's. They are brought about by himself, and not by another; and they can only be altered by himself, never by another. His condition is also his own, and not another man's. His suffering and his happiness are evolved from within. As he thinks, so he is; as he continues to think, so he remains.

A strong man cannot help a weaker unless the weaker is *willing* to be helped, and even then the weak man must become strong of himself. He must, by his own efforts, develop the strength which he admires in another. None but himself can alter his condition.

It has been usual for men to think and to say, "Many men are slaves because one is an oppressor; let us hate the oppressor." Now, however, there is among an increasing few a tendency to reverse this judgment, and to say, "One man is an oppressor because many are slaves; let us despise the slaves."

The truth is that oppressor and slave are co-operators in ignorance, and, while seeming to afflict each other, are in reality afflicting themselves. A perfect Knowledge perceives the action of law in the weakness of the oppressed and the misapplied power of the oppressor. A perfect Love, seeing the suffering, which both states entail, condemns neither; a perfect Compassion embraces both oppressor and oppressed.

He who has conquered weakness, and has put away all selfish thoughts, belongs neither to oppressor nor oppressed. He is free.

A man can only rise, conquer, and achieve by lifting up his thoughts. He can only remain weak, and abject, and miserable by refusing to lift up his thoughts.

Before a man can achieve anything, even in worldly things, he must lift his thoughts above slavish animal indulgence. He may not, in order to succeed, give up all animality and selfishness, by any means; but a portion of it must, at least, be sacrificed. A man whose first thought is bestial indulgence could neither think clearly nor plan methodically. He could not find and develop his latent resources, and would fail in any undertaking. Not having commenced manfully to control his thoughts, he is not in a position to control affairs and to adopt serious responsibilities. He is not fit to act independently and stand alone, but he is limited only by the thoughts, which he chooses.

There can be no progress, no achievement without sacrifice. A man's worldly success will be in the measure that he sacrifices his confused animal thoughts, and fixes his mind on the development of his plans, and the strengthening of his resolution and self-reliance. And the higher he lifts his thoughts, the more manly, upright, and righteous he becomes, the greater will be his success, the more blessed an enduring will be his achievements.

The universe does not favour the greedy, the dishonest, the vicious, although on the mere surface it may sometimes appear to do so; it helps the honest, the magnanimous, the virtuous. All the great Teachers of the ages have declared this in varying forms, and to prove and know it a man has but to persist in making himself more and more virtuous by lifting up his thoughts.

Intellectual achievements are the result of thought consecrated to the search for knowledge, or for the beautiful and true in life and nature. Such achievements may be sometimes connected with vanity and ambition but they are not the outcome of those characteristics. They are the natural outgrowth of long an arduous effort, and of pure and unselfish thoughts.

Spiritual achievements are the consummation of holy aspirations. He who lives constantly in the conception of noble and lofty thoughts, who dwells upon all that is pure and unselfish, will, as surely as the sun reaches its zenith and the moon its full, become wise and noble in character, and rise into a position of influence and blessedness.

Achievement, of whatever kind, is the crown of effort, the diadem of thought. By the aid of self-control, resolution, purity, righteousness, and well-directed thought a man ascends; by the aid of animality, indolence, impurity, corruption, and confusion of thought a man descends.

A man may rise to high success in the world, and even to lofty altitudes in the spiritual realm, and again descend into weakness and wretchedness by allowing arrogant, selfish, and corrupt thoughts to take possession of him.

Victories attained by right thought can only be maintained by watchfulness. Many give way when success is assured, and rapidly fall back into failure.

All achievements, whether in the business, intellectual, or spiritual world, are the result of definitely directed thought, are governed by the same law and are of the same method; the only difference lies in the *object of attainment.*

He who would accomplish little must sacrifice little. He who would achieve much must sacrifice much. He who would attain highly must sacrifice greatly.

6

VISIONS AND IDEALS

The dreamers are the saviours of the world. As the visible world is sustained by the invisible, so men, through all their trials and sins and sordid vocations, are nourished by the beautiful visions of their solitary dreamers. Humanity cannot forget its dreamers. It cannot let their ideals fade and die. It lives in them. It knows them in the *realities* which it shall one day see and know.

Composer, sculptor, painter, poet, prophet, sage, these are the makers of the after-world, the architects of heaven. The world is beautiful because they have lived; without them, labouring humanity would perish.

He who cherishes a beautiful vision, a lofty ideal in his heart, will one day realize it. Columbus cherished a vision of another world, and he discovered it. Copernicus fostered the vision of a multiplicity of worlds and a wider universe, and he revealed it. Buddha beheld the vision of a spiritual world of stainless beauty and perfect peace, and he entered into it.

Cherish your visions. Cherish your ideals. Cherish the music that stirs in your heart, the beauty that forms in your mind, the loveliness that drapes your purest thoughts, for out of them will grow all delightful conditions, all heavenly environment; of these, if you but remain true to them, your world will at last be built.

To desire is to obtain; to aspire is to achieve. Shall man's basest desires receive the fullest measure of gratification, and his purest aspirations starve for lack of sustenance? Such is not the Law. Such a condition of things can never obtain: "ask and receive."

Dream lofty dreams, and as you dream, so shall you become. Your Vision is the promise of what you shall one day be; your Ideal is the prophecy of what you shall at last unveil.

The greatest achievement was at first and for a time a dream. The oak sleeps in the acorn; the bird waits in the egg; and in the highest vision of the soul a waking angel stirs. Dreams are the seedlings of realities.

Your circumstances may be uncongenial, but they shall not long remain so if you but perceive an Ideal and strive to reach it. You cannot travel *within* and stand still *without*. Here is a youth hard pressed by poverty and labour; confined long hours in an unhealthy workshop; unschooled, and lacking all the arts of refinement. But he dreams of better things. He thinks of intelligence, of refinement, of grace and beauty. He conceives of, mentally builds up, an ideal condition of life. The vision of the wider liberty and a larger scope takes possession of him; unrest urges him to action, and he utilizes all his spare time and means, small though they are, to the development of his latent powers and resources. Very soon so altered has his mind become that the workshop can no longer hold him. It has become so out of harmony with his mentality that it falls out of his life as a garment is cast aside, and, with the growth of opportunities, which fit the scope of his expanding powers, he passes out of it forever. Years later we see this youth as a full-grown man. We find him a master of certain forces of the mind, which he wields with worldwide influence and almost unequaled power. In his hands he holds the cords of gigantic responsibilities; he speaks, and lo, lives are changed; men and women hang upon his words and remould their characters, and, sunlike, he becomes the fixed and luminous centre around which innumerable destinies revolve. He has realized the Vision of his youth. He has become one with his Ideal.

And you, too, youthful reader, will realize the Vision (not the idle wish) of your heart, be it base or beautiful, or a mixture of both, for you will always gravitate toward that which you secretly, most love. Into your hands will be placed the exact results of your own thoughts; you will receive that which you earn; no more, no less. Whatever your present environment may be, you will fall, remain, or rise with your thoughts, your Vision, your Ideal. You will become as small as your controlling desire; as great as your dominant aspiration: in the beautiful words of Stanton Kirkham Dave, "You may be keeping accounts, and presently you shall walk out of the door that for so long has seemed to you the barrier of your ideals, and shall find yourself before an audience—the pen still behind your ear, the ink stains on your fingers, and then and there shall pour out the torrent of your inspiration. You may be driving sheep, and you shall wander to the city—bucolic and open-mouthed; shall wander under the intrepid guidance of the spirit into the studio of the master, and after a time he shall say, 'I have nothing more to teach you.' And now you have become the master, who did so recently dream of great things while driving sheep. You shall lay down the saw and the plane to take upon yourself the regeneration of the world."

The thoughtless, the ignorant, and the indolent, seeing only the apparent effects of things and not the things themselves, talk of luck, of fortune, and chance. See a man grow rich, they say, "How lucky he is!" Observing another become intellectual, they exclaim, "How highly favoured he is!" And noting the saintly character and wide influence of another, they remark, "How chance aids him at every turn!" They do not see the trials and failures and struggles which these men have voluntarily encountered in order to gain their experience; have no knowledge of the sacrifices they have made, of the undaunted efforts they have put forth, of the faith they have exercised, that they might overcome the apparently insurmountable, and realize the Vision of their heart. They do not know the darkness and the heartaches; they only see the light and joy, and call it "luck"; do not see the long and arduous journey, but only behold the pleasant goal, and call it "good fortune"; do not understand the process, but only perceive the result, and call it "chance."

In all human affairs there are *efforts*, and there are *results*, and the strength of the effort is the measure of the result. Chance is not. Gifts, powers, material, intellectual, and spiritual possessions are the fruits of effort. They are thoughts completed, objects accomplished, visions realized.

The vision that you glorify in your mind, the Ideal that you enthrone in your heart—this you will build your life by, this you will become.

7

SERENITY

Calmness of mind is one of the beautiful jewels of wisdom. It is the result of long and patient effort in self-control. Its presence is an indication of ripened experience, and of a more than ordinary knowledge of the laws and operations of thought.

A man becomes calm in the measure that he understands himself as a thought-evolved being, for such knowledge necessitates the understanding of others as the result of thought, and as he develops a right understanding, and sees more and more clearly the internal relations of things by the action of cause and effect he ceases to fuss and fume and worry and grieve, and remains poised, steadfast, serene.

The calm man, having learned how to govern himself, knows how to adapt himself to others; and they, in turn, reverence his spiritual strength, and feel that they can learn of him and rely upon him. The more tranquil a man becomes, the greater is his success, his influence, his power for good. Even the ordinary trader will find his business prosperity increase as he develops a greater self-control and equanimity, for people will always prefer to deal with a man whose demeanor is strongly equable.

The strong, calm man is always loved and revered. He is like a shade-giving tree in a thirsty land, or a sheltering rock in a storm. "Who does not love a tranquil heart, a sweet-tempered, balanced life? It does not matter whether it rains or shines, or what changes come to those possessing these blessings, for they are always sweet, serene, and calm. That exquisite poise of character which we call serenity is the last lesson culture, the fruitage of the soul. It is precious as wisdom, more to be desired than gold—yea, than even fine gold. How insignificant mere money-seeking looks in comparison with a serene life—a life that dwells in the ocean of Truth, beneath the waves, beyond the reach of tempests, in the Eternal Calm!

"How many people we know who sour their lives, who ruin all that is sweet and beautiful by explosive tempers, who destroy their poise of character, and make bad blood! It is a question whether the great majority of people do not ruin their lives and mar their happiness by lack of self-control. How few people we meet in life who are well balanced, who have that exquisite poise which is characteristic of the finished character!"

Yes, humanity surges with uncontrolled passion, is tumultuous with ungoverned grief, is blown about by anxiety and doubt. Only the wise man, only he whose thoughts are controlled and purified, makes the winds and the storms of the soul obey him.

Tempest-tossed souls, wherever ye may be, under whatsoever conditions ye may live, know this: in the ocean of life the isles of Blessedness are smiling, and sunny shore of your ideal awaits your coming. Keep your hand firmly upon the helm of thought. In the bark of your soul reclines the commanding Master; He does but sleep; wake Him. Self-control is strength; Right Thought is mastery; Calmness is power. Say unto your heart, "Peace, be still!"

LIGHT ON LIFE'S DIFFICULTIES

As Published in 1912

FOREWORD

When a man enters a dark room he is not sure of his movements, he cannot see objects around him, or properly locate them, and is liable to hurt himself by coming into sudden contact with them. But let a light be introduced, and immediately all confusion disappears. Every object is seen, and there is no danger of being hurt. To the majority, life is such a dark room, and their frequent hurts—their disappointments, perplexities, sorrows and pains—are caused by sudden contact with principles which they do not see, and are therefore not prepared to deal with. But when the light of wisdom is introduced into the darkened understanding, confusion vanishes, difficulties are dissolved, all things are seen in their true place and proportion, and henceforth the man walks open-eyed and unhurt, in the clear light of wise comprehension.

James Allen

LIGHT ON FACTS
AND HYPOTHESES

When freedom of thought and freedom of expression abound, there is much controversy and much confusion. Yet it is from such controversial confusion that the simple facts of life emerge, attracting us with their eternal uniformity and harmony, and appealing forcibly to us with their invisible simplicity and truth. We are living in an age of freedom and mental conflict. Never were religious sects so numerous. Schools—philosophical, occult, and otherwise—abound, and each is eager for the perpetuation and dominance of its own explanation of the universe. The world is in a condition of mental ferment. Contradiction has reached the point of confusion, so that the earnest seeker for Truth can find no solid rock of refuge in the opposing systems which are presented to him. He is thereby thrown back upon himself, upon those incontrovertible facts of his own being which are ever with him—which are, indeed, himself, his life.

Controversy is ranged around hypotheses, not around facts. Fact is fixed and final; hypothesis is variable and vanishing. In his present stage of development, man is not alive to the beautiful simplicity of facts, nor to the power of satisfaction which is inherent in them. He does not perceive the intrinsic loveliness of truth, but must add something to it.

Hence, when fact is named, the question almost invariably arises, "How can you explain the fact?" and then follows a hypothesis which leads to another hypothesis, and so on and on until the fact is altogether lost sight of amid a mass of contradictory suppositions. Thus arise the sects and controversial schools.

The clear perception of one fact will lead to the perception of other facts, but a supposition, while appearing to elucidate a fact, does in reality cover it up. We cannot realize the stately splendor of Truth while playing with the gaudy and attractive toys of pretty hypotheses. Truth is not an opinion, nor can any opinion enlarge or adorn it. Fact and supposition are eternally separate, and the cleverest intellectual jugglery—while it may entertain and deceive even the elect—cannot in the slightest degree alter a fact or affect the nature of things-as-they-are. Because of this, the true teacher abandons the devious path of hypothesis, and deals only with the simple facts of life. He fixes the attention of men and women upon these, instead of increasing confusion and intensifying wordy warfare by foisting another assumption upon a world already lost and bewildered in a maze of hypotheses.

The facts of life are ever before us, and can be understood and known if we but abandon our egotism and the blinding delusions which that egotism creates. Man need not go beyond his own being to find wisdom, and the facts of that being afford a sufficient basis on which to erect a temple of knowledge of such beauty and dimensions that it shall at once emancipate and glorify.

Man is; and as he thinks, so he is. A perception and realization of these two facts alone—of man's being and thinking—lead into a vast avenue of knowledge which cannot stop short of the highest wisdom and perfection. One of the reasons why men do not become wise is that they occupy themselves with interminable speculations about a soul separate from themselves—that is, from their own mind—and so blind themselves to their actual nature and being. The supposition of a separate soul veils the eyes of man so that he does not see himself, does not know his mentality, is unaware of the nature of his thoughts without which he would have no conscious life.

Man's life is actual; his thoughts are actual; his life is actual. To occupy ourselves with the investigation of things that are is the way of wisdom. Man considered as above, beyond, and separate from mind and thought, is speculative and not actual, and to occupy ourselves with the study of things that are not, is the way of folly.

Man cannot be separated from his mind; his life cannot be separated from his thoughts. Mind, thought, and life are as inseparable as light, radiance, and color, and are no more in need of another factor to elucidate them than are light, radiance, and color. The facts are all-sufficient and contain within themselves the groundwork of all knowledge concerning them.

Man as mind is subject to change. He is not something "made" and finally completed, but has within him the capacity for progress. By the universal law of evolution he has become what he is, and is becoming that which he will be. His being is modified by every thought he thinks. Every experience affects his character. Every effort he makes changes his mentality. Herein is the secret of man's degradation, and also of his power and salvation if he but utilize this law of change in the right choice of thought.

To live is to think and act, and to think and act is to change. While man is ignorant of the nature of thought, he continues to change for better and worse; but, being acquainted with the nature of thought, he intelligently accelerates and directs the process of change, and only for the better.

What the sum total of a man's thoughts are, that he is. From this sameness of thought with man there is not the slightest fractional deviation. There is a change as a result with the addition and subtraction of thought, but the mathematical law is an invariable quality.

Seeing that man is mind, that mind is composed of thought, and that thought is subject to change, it follows that deliberately to change the thought is to change the man.

All religions work upon the heart, the thought of man, with the object of directing it into purer and higher channels. Success in this direction, whether partial or complete, is called "salvation"—that is, deliverance from one kind of thought, one condition of mind, by the substitution of another thought, another condition.

It is true that the dispensers of religion today do not know this because of the hypothetical veil which intervenes between the fact and their consciousness. But they do it without knowing it, and the Great Teachers who founded the various religions, built upon this fact, as their precepts plainly show. The chief things upon which these Teachers lay such stress, and so constantly reiterate—such as the purification of the heart, the thinking of right thoughts, and the doing of good deeds—what are they but calls to a higher, nobler mode of thought-energizing forces urging men and women to make an effort in the choosing of thoughts which shall lift them into realms of greater power, greater good, greater bliss?

Aspiration, meditation, devotion—these are the chief means which men in all ages employ to reach up to higher modes of thought, wider airs of peace, vaster realms of knowledge, for "as he thinketh in his heart, so is he." He is saved from himself—from his own folly and suffering—by creating within new habits of thoughts, by becoming a new thinker, a new man.

Should a man by a supreme effort succeed in thinking as Jesus thought—not by imitation, but by a sudden realization of his indwelling power—he would be as Jesus.

In the Buddhistic records there is an instance of a man, not the possessor of great piety or wisdom, who asked Buddha how one might attain the highest wisdom and enlightenment. Buddha replied, "By ceasing all desire." It is recorded that the man let go of all personal desires and at once realized the highest wisdom and enlightenment.

One of the sayings of Buddha runs, "The only miracle with which the wise man concerns himself is the transformation of a sinner into a saint." Emerson also referred to this transforming power of change of thought when he said: "It is as easy to be great as to be small," which is closely akin to that other great and oft-repeated but little understood saying; "Be ye therefore perfect, even as your Father which is in Heaven is perfect."

And, after all, what is the fundamental difference between a great man and a small one? It is one of thought, of mental attitude. True, it is one of knowledge, but then, knowledge cannot be separated from thought. Every substitution of a better for a worse thought is a transforming agency which marks an important advance in knowledge. Throughout the whole range of human life, from the lowest savage to the highest type of man, thought determines character, condition, knowledge.

The mass of humanity moves slowly along the evolutionary path urged by the blind impulse of its dominant thoughts as they are stimulated and called forth by external things. But the true thinker, the sage, travels swiftly and intelligently along a chosen path of his own. The multitudes, unenlightened concerning their spiritual nature, are the slaves of thought, but the sage is the master of thought. They follow blindly, he chooses intelligently. They obey the impulse of the moment, thinking of their immediate pleasure and happiness; he commands and subdues impulse, resting upon that which is permanently right. They, obeying blind impulse, violate the laws of righteousness; he, conquering impulse, obeys the law of righteousness. The sage stands face to face with the facts of life. He knows the nature of thought. He understands and obeys the law of his being.

But the sorrow-burdened victim of blind impulse can open his mental eyes and see the true nature of things when he wishes to do so. The sage—intelligent, radiant, calm—and the fool—confused, darkened, disturbed—are one in essence, and are divided only by the nature of their thoughts. When the fool turns away from and abandons his foolish thoughts and chooses and adopts wise thoughts, lo! he becomes a sage.

Socrates saw the essential oneness of virtue and knowledge, and so every sage sees. Learning may aid and accompany wisdom, but it does not lead to it. Only the choosing of wise thoughts, and, necessarily, the doing of wise deeds, leads to wisdom. A man may be learned in the schools, but foolish in the school of life. Not the committing of words to memory, but the establishing of oneself in purer thoughts, nobler thinking, leads to the peace-giving revelations of true knowledge.

Folly and wisdom, ignorance and enlightenment, are not merely the result of thought, they are thought itself. Both cause and effect—effort and result—are contained in thought.

All that we are is the result of what we have thought.
It is founded on our thoughts; it is made up of our thoughts.

Man is not a being possessing a soul. He himself is soul. He himself is the thinker and doer, actor and knower. His composite mentality is himself. His spiritual nature is rounded by his sphere of thought. He it is that desires and sorrows, enjoys and suffers, loves and hates. The mind is not the instrument of a metaphysical, superhuman soul. Man is soul; mind is being; mind is man.

Man can find himself. He can see himself as he is. When he is prepared to turn from the illusory and self-created world of hypothesis in which he wanders and to stand face to face with actuality, then will he know himself as he is. Moreover, he can picture himself as he would wish to be, and he can create within him the new thinker, the new man. For every moment is the time of choice—and every hour is destiny.

ABOVE LIFE'S TURMOIL

As Published in 1910

FOREWORD

We cannot alter external things, nor shape other people to our liking, nor mould the world to our wishes but we can alter internal things—our desires, passions, thoughts—we can shape our liking to other people, and we can mould the inner world of our own mind in accordance with wisdom, and so reconcile it to the outer world if men and things. The turmoil of the world we cannot avoid, but the distur - bances of mind we can overcome. The duties and difficulties of life claim our attention, but we can rise above all anxiety concerning them. Surrounded by noise, we can yet have a quiet mind; involved in responsi- bilities, the heart can be at rest; in the midst of strife, we can know the abiding peace. The twenty pieces which comprise this book, unrelated as some of them are in the letter, will be found to be harmonious in the spirit, in that they point the reader towards those heights of self-knowledge and self-conquest which, rising above the turbulence of the world, lift their peaks where the Heavenly Silence reigns.

James Allen

1

True Happiness

To maintain an unchangeable sweetness of disposition, to think only thoughts that are pure and gentle, and to be happy under all circumstances—such blessed conditions and such beauty of character and life should be the aim of all, and particularly so of those who wish to lessen the misery of the world. If anyone has failed to lift *himself* above ungentleness, impurity, and unhappiness, he is greatly deluded if he imagines he can make the world happier by the propagation of any theory or theology. He who is daily living in harshness, impurity, or unhappiness is day by day adding to the sum of the world's misery; whereas he who continually lives in goodwill, and does not depart from happiness, is day by day increasing the sum of the world's happiness, and this independ-ently of any religious beliefs which these may or may not hold.

He who has not learned how to be gentle, or giving, loving and happy, has learned very little, great though his book-learning and profound his acquaintance which the letter of Scripture may be, for it is in the process of *becoming* gentle, pure, and happy that the deep, real and enduring lessons of life are learned. Unbroken sweetness of conduct in the face of all outward antagonism is the infallible indication of a self-conquered soul, the witness of wisdom, and the proof of the possession of Truth.

A sweet and happy soul is the ripened fruit of experience and wisdom, and it sheds abroad the invisible yet powerful aroma of its influence, gladdening the hearts of others, and purifying the world. And all who will, and who have not yet commenced, may begin *this* day, if they will so resolve, to live sweetly and happily, as becomes the dignity of a true manhood or womanhood. Do not say that your surroundings are against you. A man's surroundings are never against him; they are there to aid him, and all those outward occurrences over which you lose sweetness and peace of mind are the very conditions necessary to your development, and it is only by meeting and overcoming them that you can learn, and grow, and ripen. The fault is in yourself.

Pure happiness is the rightful and healthy condition of the soul, and all may possess it if they will live purely and unselfish.

> *Have goodwill*
> *To all that lives, letting unkindness die,*
> *And greed and wrath, so that your lives be made*
> *Like soft airs passing by.*

Is this too difficult for you? Then unrest and unhappiness will continue to dwell with you. Your belief and aspiration and resolve are all that are necessary to make it easy, to render it in the near future a thing accomplished, a blessed state realised.

Despondency, irritability, anxiety and complaining, condemning and grumbling—all these are thought-cankers, mind-diseases; they are the indications of a wrong mental condition, and those who suffer therefrom would do well to remedy their thinking and conduct. It is true there is much sin and misery in the world, so that all our love and compassion are needed, but our misery is not needed—there is already too much of that. No, it is our cheerfulness and happiness that are needed for there is too little of that. We can give nothing better to the world than beauty of life and character; without this, all other things are vain; this is pre-eminently excellent; it is enduring, real, and not to be overthrown, and it includes all joy and blessedness.

Cease to dwell pessimistically upon the wrongs around you; dwell no more in complaints about, and revolt against, the evil in others, and commence to live free from all wrong and evil yourself. Peace of mind, pure religion, and true reform lie this way. If you would have others true, be true; if you would have the world emancipated from misery and sin, emancipate yourself; if you would have your home and your surroundings happy, be happy. You can transform everything around you if you will transform yourself.

> *Don't bewail and bemoan . . .*
> *Don't waste yourself in rejection, nor bark against the bad,*
> *but chant the beauties of the good.*

And this you will naturally and spontaneously do as you realise the good in yourself.

2

THE IMMORTAL MAN

Immortality is here and now, and is not a speculative something beyond the grave. It is a lucid state of consciousness in which the sensations of the body, the varying and unrestful states of mind, and the circumstances and events of life are seen to be of a fleeting and therefore of an illusory character.

Immortality does not belong to time, and will never be found in time; it belongs to Eternity; and just as time is here and now, so is Eternity here and now, and a man may find that Eternity and establish in it, if he will overcome the self that derives its life from the unsatisfying and perishable things of time.

Whilst a man remains immersed in sensation, desire, and the passing events of his day-by-day existence, and regards those sensations, desires, and passing events as of the essence of himself, he can have no knowledge of immortality. The thing which such a man desires, and which he mistakes for immortality, is *persistence*; that is, a continuous succession of sensations and events in time. Living in, loving and clinging to, the things which stimulate and minister to his immediate gratification, and realising no state of consciousness above and independent of this, he thirsts for its continuance, and strives to banish the thought that he will at last have to part from those earthly luxuries and delights to which he has become enslaved, and which he regards as being inseparable from himself.

Persistence is the antithesis of immortality; and to be absorbed in it is spiritual death. Its very nature is change, impermanence. It is a continual living and dying.

The death of the body can never bestow upon a man immortality. Spirits are not different from men, and live their little feverish life of broken consciousness, and are still immersed in change and mortality. The mortal man, he who thirsts for the persistence of his pleasure-loving personality, is still mortal after death, and only lives another life with a beginning and an end without memory of the past, or knowledge of the future.

The immortal man is he who has detached himself from the things of time by having ascended into that state of consciousness which is fixed and unvariable, and is not affected by passing events and sensations. Human life consists of an evermoving procession of events, and in this procession the mortal man is immersed, and he is carried along with it; and being so carried along, he has no knowledge of what is behind and before him. The immortal man is he who has stepped out of this procession, and he stands by unmoved and watches it; and from his fixed place he sees both the before, the behind and the middle of the moving thing called life. No longer identifying himself with the sensations and fluctuations of the personality, or with the outward changes which make up the life in time, he has become the passionless spectator of his own destiny and of the destinies of the men and nations.

The mortal man, also, is one who is caught in a dream, and he neither knows that he was formerly awake, nor that he will wake again; he is a dreamer without knowledge, nothing more. The immortal man is as one who has awakened out of his dream, and he knows that his dream was not an enduring reality, but a passing illusion. He is a man with knowledge, the knowledge of both states—that of persistence, and that of immortality—and is in full possession of himself.

The mortal man lives in the time or world state of consciousness which begins and ends; the immortal man lives in the cosmic or heaven state of consciousness, in which there is neither beginning nor end, but an eternal now. Such a man remains poised and steadfast under all changes, and the death of his body will not in any way interrupt the eternal consciousness in which he abides. Of such a one it is said, "He shall not taste of death," because he has stepped out of the stream of mortality, and established himself in the abode of Truth. Bodies, personalities, nations, and worlds pass away, but Truth remains, and its glory is undimmed by time. The immortal man, then, is he who has conquered himself; who no longer identifies himself with the self-seeking forces of the personality, but who has trained himself to direct those forces with the hand of a master, and so has brought them into harmony with the causal energy and source of all things.

The fret and fever of life has ceased, doubt and fear are cast out, and death is not for him who has realised the fadeless splendour of that life of Truth by adjusting heart and mind to the eternal and unchangeable verities.

ing quality. For instance, when a man is tempted to irri-
nd by a great effort overcomes the selfish tendency, casts
cts from the spirit of patience and love, in that moment
he practises the annihilation of self. Every noble man
t, though he may deny it in his words, and he who
ractice to its completion, eradicating every selfish ten-
the divinely beautiful qualities remain, he is said to have
rsonality (all the personal elements) and to have arrived
which is to be annihilated is composed of the following
sorrow-producing elements:

abandonment, the complete annihilation of these ten
y comprise the body of desire. On the other hand it
ation, practice, and preservation of the following ten

THE OVER

and peace-produ
tability or anger,
it from him, and
of self-conquest
practises it in p
carries out this
dency until only
annihilated the p
at Truth. The sel
ten worthless an

- Lust
- Vanity
- Hatred
- Pride
- Avarice
- Doubt
- Self-indulgenc
- Dark belief
- Self-seeking
- Delusion

M any people have ver
the terms "the ove
and "the annihilation of th
lectual who are prone to
altogether apart from life a
the crushing out of all li
idealise stagnation and de
they do in the minds of in
viduals themselves; but pe
difficult (for those who are
another way.

The doctrine of the o
itself; indeed, so simple, pr
five, whose mind has not y
schemes and speculative ph
prehend it than many olde
and beautiful truths by the

The annihilation of se
those elements in the soul
and sorrow. It does not me

It is the tota
elements, for the
teaches the culti
divine qualities:

- Purity
- Fearlessness
- Patience
- Knowledge
- Humility
- Wisdom
- Self-sacrifice

- Compassion
- Self-reliance
- Love

These comprise the Body of Truth, and to live entirely in them is to be a doer and knower of the Truth, is to be an embodiment of Truth. The combination of the ten elements is called Self or the Personality; the combination of the ten qualities produces what is called Truth; the Impersonal; the abiding, real and immortal Man.

It will thus be seen that it is not the destruction of any noble, true, and enduring quality that is taught, but only the destruction of those things that are ignoble, false and evanescent. Neither is this overcoming of self the deprivation of gladness, happiness and joy, but rather is it the constant possession of these things by living in the joy-begetting qualities. It is the abandonment of the lust for enjoyment, but not of enjoyment itself; the destruction of the *thirst* for pleasure, but not of pleasure itself; the annihilation of the *selfish longing* for love, and power, and possessions themselves. It is the preservation of all those things which draw and bind men together in unity and concord, and, far from idealising stagnation and death, urges men to the practice of those qualities which lead to the highest, noblest, most effective, and enduring action. He whose actions proceed from some or all of the ten elements wastes his energies upon negations, and does not preserve his soul; but he whose actions proceed from some or all of the ten qualities, he truly and wisely acts and so preserves his soul.

He who lives largely in the ten earthly elements, and who is blind and deaf to the spiritual verities, will find no attraction in the doctrine of self-surrender, for it will appear to him as the complete extinction of his being; but he who is endeavouring to live in the ten heavenly qualities will see the glory and beauty of the doctrine, and will know it as the foundation of Life Eternal. He will also see that when men apprehend and practise it, industry, commerce, government, and every worldly activity will be purified; and action, purpose and intelligence, instead of being destroyed, will be intensified and enlarged, but freed from strife and pain.

4

THE USES OF TEMPTATION

The soul, in its journey towards perfection, passes through three distinct stages. The first is the *animal* stage, in which the man is content to live, in the gratification of his senses, unawakened to the knowledge of sin, or of his divine inheritance, and altogether unconscious of the spiritual possibilities within himself.

The second is the *dual* stage, in which the mind is continually oscillating between its animal and divine tendencies having become awakened to the consciousness of both. It is during this stage that temptation plays its part in the progress of the soul. It is a stage of continual fighting, of falling and rising, of sinning and repenting, for the man, still loving, and reluctant to leave, the gratifications in which he has so long lived, yet also aspires to the purity and excellence of the spiritual state, and he is continually mortified by an undecided choice.

Urged on by the divine life within him, this stage becomes at last one of deep anguish and suffering, and then the soul is ushered into the third stage, that of *knowledge*, in which the man rises above both sin and temptation, and enters into peace.

Temptation, like contentment in sin, is not a lasting condition, as the majority of people suppose; it is a passing phase, an experience through which the soul must pass; but as to whether a man will pass through that condition in this present life, and realise holiness and heavenly rest here and now, will depend entirely upon the strength of his intellectual and spiritual exertions, and upon the intensity and ardour with which he searches for Truth.

Temptation, with all its attendant torments can be overcome here and now, but it can only be overcome by knowledge. It is a condition of darkness or of semi-darkness. The fully enlightened soul is proof against all temptation. When a man fully understands the source, nature, and meaning of temptation, in that hour he will conquer it, and will rest from his long travail; but whilst he remains in ignorance, attention to religious observances, and much praying and reading of Scripture will fail to bring him peace.

If a man goes out to conquer an enemy, knowing nothing of his enemy's strength, tactics, or place of ambush, he will not only ignomin-iously fail, but will speedily fall into the hands of the enemy. He who would overcome his enemy the tempter, must discover his stronghold and place of concealment, and must also find out the unguarded gates in his own fortress where his enemy effects so easy an entrance. This necessitates continual meditation, ceaseless watchfulness, and constant and rigid introspection which lays bare, before the spiritual eyes of the tempted one, the vain and selfish motives of his soul. This is the holy warfare of the saints; it is the fight upon which every soul enters when it awakens out of its long sleep of animal indulgence.

Men fail to conquer, and the fight is indefinitely prolonged, because they labour, almost universally, under two delusions: first, that all temptations come from without; and second, that they are tempted because of their goodness. Whilst a man is held in bondage by these two delusions, he will make no progress; when he has shaken them off, he will pass on rapidly from victory to victory, and will taste of spiritual joy and rest.

Two searching truths must take the place of these two delusions, and those truths are: first, that all temptation comes from within; and second, that a man is tempted because of the evil that is within him. The idea that God, a devil, evil spirits, or outward objects are the source of temptation must be dispelled. The source and cause of all temptation is in the inward desire; that being purified or eliminated, outward objects and extraneous powers are utterly powerless to move the soul to sin or to temptation. The outward object is merely the occasion of the temptation, never the cause; this is in the desire of the one tempted. If the cause existed in the object, all men would be tempted alike, temptation could never be overcome, and men would be hopelessly doomed to endless torment; but seated, as it is, in his own desires, he has the remedy in his own hands, and can become victorious over all temptation by purifying those desires. A man is tempted because there are within him certain desires or states of mind which he has come to regard as unholy. These desires may lie asleep for a long time, and the man may think that he has got rid of them, when suddenly, on the presentation of an outward object, the sleeping desire wakes up and thirsts of immediate gratification; and this is the state of temptation.

The good in a man is never tempted. Goodness destroys temptation. It is the evil in a man that is aroused and tempted. The measure of a man's temptations is the exact register of his own unholiness. As a man purifies his heart, temptation ceases, for when a certain unlawful desire has been taken out of the heart, the object which formerly appealed to it can no longer do so, but becomes dead and powerless, for there is nothing left in the heart that can respond to it. The honest man cannot be tempted to steal, let the occasion be ever so opportune; the man of purified appetites cannot be tempted to gluttony and drunkenness, though the viands and wines be the most luscious; he of an enlightened understanding, whose mind is calm in the strength of inward virtue, can never be tempted to anger, irritability or revenge, and the wiles and charms of the wanton fall upon the purified heart as empty meaningless shadows.

Temptation shows a man just where he is sinful and ignorant, and is a means of urging him on to higher altitudes of knowledge and purity. Without temptation the soul cannot grow and become strong, there could be no wisdom, no real virtue; and though there would be lethargy and death, there could be no peace and no fullness of life. When temptation is understood and conquered, perfection is assured, and such perfection may become any man's who is willing to cast every selfish and impure desire by which he is possessed, into the sacrificial fire of knowledge. Let men, therefore, search diligently for Truth, realising that whilst they are subject to temptation, they have not comprehended Truth, and have much to learn.

Ye who are tempted know, then, that ye are tempted of yourselves. "For every man is tempted when he is drawn away of his own lusts," says the Apostle James. You are tempted because you are clinging to the animal within you and are unwilling to let go; because you are living in the false mortal self which is ever devoid of all true knowledge, knowing nothing, seeking nothing, but its own immediate gratification, ignorant of every Truth, and of every divine Principle. Clinging to that self, you continually suffer the pains of three separate torments: the torment of desire, the torment of repletion, and the torment of remorse.

> *So flameth Trishna, lust and thirst of things.*
> *Eager, ye cleave to shadows, dote on dreams;*
> *A false self in the midst ye plant, and make*
> *A World around which seems;*
> *Blind to the height beyond; deaf to the sound*
> *Of sweet airs breathed from far past Indra's sky;*
> *Dumb to the summons of the true life kept*
> *For him who false puts by,*
> *So grow the strifes and lusts which make earth's war,*
> *So grieve poor cheated hearts and flow salt tears;*
> *So wax the passions, envies, angers, hates;*
> *So years chase blood-stained years*
> *With wild red feet.*

In that false self lies the germ of every suffering, the blight of every hope, the substance of every grief. When you are ready to give it up; when you are willing to have laid bare before you all its selfishness, impurity, and ignorance, and to confess its darkness to the uttermost, then will you enter upon the life of self-knowledge and self-mastery;

you will become conscious of the god within you, of that divine nature which, seeking no gratification, abides in a region of perpetual joy and peace where suffering cannot come and where temptation can find no foothold. Establishing yourself, day by day, more and more firmly in that inward Divinity, the time will at last come when you will be able to say with Him whom millions worship, few understand and fewer still follow—"The Prince of this world cometh and hath nothing in me."

5

THE MAN OF INTEGRITY

There are times in the life of every man who takes his stand on high moral principles when his faith in, and knowledge of, those principles is tested to the uttermost, and the way in which he comes out of the fiery trial decides as to whether he has sufficient strength to live as a man of Truth, and join the company of the free, or shall still remain a slave and a hireling to the cruel taskmaster, Self.

Such times of trial generally assume the form of a temptation to do a wrong thing and continue in comfort and prosperity, or to stand by what is right and accept poverty and failure; and so powerful is the trial that, to the tempted one, it plainly appears on the face of things as though, if he chooses the wrong, his material success will be assured for the remainder of his life, but if he does what is right, he will be ruined for ever.

Frequently the man at once quails and gives way before this appalling prospect which the Path of Righteousness seems to hold out for him, but should he prove sufficiently strong to withstand this onslaught of temptation, then the inward seducer the spirit of self, assumes the grab of an Angel of Light, and whispers, "Think of your wife and children; think of those who are dependent upon you; will you bring them down to disgrace and starvation?"

Strong indeed and pure must be the man who can come triumphant out of such a trial, but he who does so, enters at once a higher realm of life, where his spiritual eyes are opened to see beautiful things; and then poverty and ruin which seemed inevitable do not come, but a more abiding success comes, and a peaceful heart and a quiet conscience. But he who fails does not obtain the promised prosperity, and his heart is restless and his conscience troubled.

The right-doer cannot ultimately fail, the wrong-doer cannot ultimately succeed, for:

> *Such is the Law which moves to Righteousness*
> *Which none at last can turn aside or stay,*

and it is because justice is at the heart of things—because the Great Law is good that the man of integrity is superior to fear, and failure, and poverty, and shame, and disgrace. As the poet further says of this Law:

> *The heart of its Love, the end of it*
> *Is peace and consummation sweet-obey.*

The man who fearing the loss of present pleasures or material comforts, denies the Truth within him, can be injured, and robbed, and degraded, and trampled upon, because he has first injured, robbed and degraded, and trampled upon his own nobler self; but the man of steadfast virtue, of unblemished integrity, cannot be subject to such conditions, because he has denied the craven self within him and has taken refuge in Truth. It is not the scourge and the chains which make a man a slave, but the fact that he *is* a slave.

Slander, accusation, and malice cannot affect the righteous man, nor call from him any bitter response, nor does he need to go about to defend himself and prove his innocence. His innocence and integrity alone are a sufficient answer to all that hatred may attempt against him. Nor can he ever be subdued by the forces of darkness, having subdued all those forces within himself; but he turns all evil things to good account—out of darkness he brings light, out of hatred love, out of dishonour honour; and slanders, envies, and misrepresentations only serve to make more bright the jewel of Truth within him, and to glorify his high and holy destiny.

Let the man of integrity rejoice and be glad when he is severely tried; let him be thankful that he has been given an opportunity of proving his loyalty to the noble principles which he has espoused; and let him think: "Now is the hour of holy opportunity! Now is the day of triumph for Truth! Though I lose the whole world I will not desert the right!" So thinking, he will return good for evil, and will think compassionately of the wrong-doer.

The slanderer, the backbiter, and the wrong-doer may seem to succeed for a time, but the Law of Justice prevails; the man of integrity may seem to fail for a time, but he is invincible, and in none of the worlds, visible or invisible, can there be forged a weapon that shall prevail against him.

6

DISCRIMINATION

There is one quality which is pre-eminently necessary to spiritual development, the quality of discrimination.

A man's spiritual progress will be painfully slow and uncertain until there opens with him the eye of discrimination, for without this testing, proving, searching quality, he will but grope in the dark, will be unable to distinguish the real from the unreal, the shadow from the substance, and will so confuse the false with the true as to mistake the inward promptings of his animal nature for those of the spirit of Truth.

A blind man left in a strange place may go grope his way in darkness, but not without much confusion and many painful falls and bruisings. Without discrimination a man is mentally blind, and his life is a painful groping in darkness, a confusion in which vice and virtue are indistinguishable one from the other, where facts are confounded with truths; opinions with principles, and where ideas, events, men, and things appear to be out of all relation to each other. A man's mind and life should be free from confusion. He should be prepared to meet every mental, material and spiritual difficulty, and should not be inextricably caught (as many are) in the meshes of doubt, indecision and uncertainty when troubles and so-called misfortunes come along. He should be for-tified against every emergency that can come against him; but such mental preparedness and strength cannot be attained in any degree without discrimination, and discrimination can only be developed by bringing into play and constantly exercising the analytical faculty.

Mind, like muscle, is developed by use, and the assiduous exercise of the mind in any given direction will develop, in that direction, mental capacity and power. The merely critical faculty is developed and strengthened by continuously comparing and analysing the ideas and opinions of others. But discrimination is something more and greater than criticism; it is a spiritual quality from which the cruelty and egotism which so frequently accompany criticism are eliminated, and by virtue of which a man sees things as they are, and not as he would like them to be.

Discrimination, being a spiritual quality, can only be developed by spiritual methods, namely, by questioning, examining, and analysing one's own ideas, opinions, and conduct. The critical, fault finding faculty must be withdrawn from its merciless application to the opinions and conduct of others, and must be applied, with undiminished severity, to oneself. A man must be prepared to question his every opinion, his every thought, and his every line of conduct, and rigorously and logically test them; only in this way can the discrimination which destroys confusion will be developed.

Before a man can enter upon such mental exercise, he must make himself of a teachable spirit. This does not mean that he must allow himself to be led by others; it means that he must be prepared to yield up any cherished thoughts to which he clings, if it will not bear the penetrating light of reason, if it shrivels up before the pure flames of searching aspirations. The man who says, "I am right!" and who refuses to question his position in order to discover whether he is right, will continue to follow the line of his passions and prejudices, and will not acquire discrimination. The man who humbly asks, "Am I right?" and then proceeds to test and prove his position by earnest thought and the love of Truth, will always be able to discover the true and to distinguish it from the false, and he will acquire the priceless possession of discrimination.

The man who is afraid to think searchingly upon his opinions, and to reason critically upon his position, will have to develop moral courage before he can acquire discrimination.

A man must be true to himself, fearless with himself, before he can perceive the Pure Principles of Truth, before he can receive the all-revealing Light of Truth. The more Truth is inquired of, the brighter it shines; it cannot suffer under examination and analysis.

The more error is questioned, the darker it grows; it cannot survive the entrance of pure and searching thought. To "prove all things" is to find the good and throw the evil. He who reasons and meditates learns to discriminate; he who discriminates discovers the eternally True.

Confusion, suffering and spiritual darkness follow the thoughtless.

Harmony, blessedness and the Light of Truth attend upon the thoughtful.

Passion and prejudice are blind, and cannot discriminate: they are still crucifying *the Christ* and releasing *Barabbas*.

7

BELIEF, THE BASIS OF ACTION

B elief is an important word in the teachings of the wise, and it figures prominently in all religions. According to Jesus, a certain kind of belief is necessary to salvation or regeneration, and Buddha definitely taught that right belief is the first and most essential step in the Way of Truth, as without right belief there cannot be right conduct, and he who has not learned how to rightly govern and conduct himself, has not yet comprehended the simplest rudiments of Truth.

Belief as laid down by the Great Teachers, is not belief in any particular school, philosophy, or religion, but consists of an *altitude of mind determining the whole course of one's life*. Belief and conduct are, therefore inseparable, for the one determines the other.

Belief is the basis of all action, and, this being so, the belief which dominates the hearts or mind is shown in the life. Every man acts, thinks, lives in exact accordance with the belief which is rooted in his innermost being, and such is the mathematical nature of the laws which govern mind that it is absolutely impossible for anyone to believe in two opposing conditions at the same time. For instance, it is impossible to believe in justice and injustice, hatred and love, peace and strife, self and truth. Every man believes in one or the other of these opposites, *never in both*, and the daily conduct of every man indicates the nature of his belief. The man who believes in justice, who regards it as an eternal and indestructible Principle, never boils over with righteous indignation, does not grow cynical and pessimistic over the inequalities of life, and remains calm and untroubled through all trials and difficulties. It is impossible for him to act otherwise, for he believes that justice reigns, and that, therefore, all that is called injustice is fleeting and illusory.

The man who is continually getting enraged over the injustice of his fellow men, who talks about himself being badly treated, or who mourns over the lack of justice in the world around him, shows by his conduct, his attitude of mind, that he believes in injustice. However he may protest to the contrary, in his inmost heart he believes that confusion and chaos are dominant in the universe, the result being that he dwells in misery and unrest, and his conduct is faulty.

Again, he who believes in love, in its stability and power, *practises it under all circumstances*, never deviates from it, and bestows it alike upon enemies as upon friends. He who slanders and condemns, who speaks disparagingly of others, or regards them with contempt, believes not in love, but hatred; all his actions prove it, even though with tongue or pen he may eulogise love.

The believer in peace is known by his peaceful conduct. It is impossible for him to engage in strife. If attacked he does not retaliate, for he has seen the majesty of the angel of peace, and he can no longer pay homage to the demon of strife. The stirrer-up of strife, the lover of argument, he who rushes into self-defence upon any or every provocation, believes in strife, and will have naught to do with peace.

Further, he who believes in Truth renounces himself—that is, he refuses to centre his life in those passions, desires, and characteristics which crave only their own gratification, and by thus renouncing he becomes steadfastly fixed in Truth, and lives a wise, beautiful, and blameless life. The believer in self is known by his daily indulgences, gratifications, and vanities, and by the disappointments, sorrows, and mortifications which he continually suffers.

The believer in Truth does not suffer, for he has given up that self which is the cause of such suffering.

It will be seen by the foregoing that every man believes either in permanent and eternal Principles directing human life towards law and harmony, or in the negation of those Principles, with the resultant chaos in human affairs and in his own life.

Belief in the divine Principles of Justice, Compassion, Love, constitutes the *right belief* laid down by Buddha as being the basis of *right conduct*, and also the *belief unto salvation* as emphasised in the Christian Scriptures, for he who so believes cannot do otherwise than build his whole life upon these Principles, and so purifies his heart, and perfects his life.

Belief in the negation of this divine principle constitutes what is called in all religious unbelief and this unbelief is manifested as a sinful, troubled, and imperfect life.

Where there is Right Belief there is a blameless and perfect life; where there is false belief there is sin, there is sorrow, the mind and life are improperly governed, and there is affliction and unrest. "By their fruits ye shall know them."

There is much talk about, "belief in Jesus," but what does belief in Jesus mean? It means belief in his words, in the Principles he enunciated—and lived—in his commandments and in his exemplary life of perfection. He who declares belief in Jesus, and yet is all the time living in his lusts and indulgences, or in the spirit of hatred and condemnation, is self deceived. He believes not in Jesus. He believes in his own animal self. As a faithful servant delights in carrying out the commands of his master, so he who believes in Jesus carries out his commandments, and so is saved from sin. The supreme test of belief in Jesus is this: *Do I keep his commandments?* And this test is applied by St. John himself in the following words: "He that saith. I know him (Jesus), and *keepeth not His Commandments*, is a liar, and the truth is not in him. But whoso keepeth his word, in him verily is the word of God perfected."

It will be found after a rigid and impartial analysis, that *belief* lies at the root of all human conduct. Every thought, every act, every habit, is the direct outcome of a certain fixed belief, and one's conduct alters only as one's belief are modified. What we cling to, in that we believe;

what we practise, in that we believe. When our belief in a thing ceases, we can no longer cling to or practise it; it falls away from us as a garment out-worn. Men cling to their lusts, and lies, and vanities, because they believe in them, believe there is gain and happiness in them. When they transfer their belief to the divine qualities of purity and humility, those sins trouble them no more.

Men are saved from error by belief in the supremacy of Truth. They are saved from sin by belief in Holiness or Perfection. They are saved from evil by belief in Good, for every belief is manifested in the life. It is not necessary to inquire as to a man's theological belief, for that is of little or no account, for what can it avail a man to believe that Jesus died for him, or that Jesus is God, or that he is "justified by faith," if he continues to live in his lower, sinful nature? All that is necessary to ask is this: "How does a man live?" "How does he conduct himself under trying circumstances?" The answer to these questions will show whether a man believes in the power of evil or in the power of Good.

He who believes in the power of Good, lives a good, spiritual, or godly life, for Goodness is God, yea, verily is God Himself, and he will soon leave behind him all sins and sorrows who believes, with steadfast and unwavering faith, in the Supreme Good.

8

BELIEF THAT SAVES

It has been said that a man's whole life and character is the outcome of his *belief,* and also that his *belief* has nothing whatever to do with his life. *Both statements are true.* The confusion and contradiction of these two statements are only apparent, and are quickly dispelled when it is remembered that there are *two entirely distinct kinds of beliefs,* namely, Head-belief and Heart-belief.

Head, or intellectual belief, is not fundamental and causative, but it is superficial and consequent, and that it has no power in the moulding of a man's character, the most superficial observer may easily see. Take, for instance, half a dozen men from any creed. They not only hold the same theological belief, but confess the same articles of faith in every particular, and yet their characters are vastly different. One will be just as noble as another is ignoble; one will be mild and gentle, another coarse and irascible; one will be honest, another dishonest; one will indulge certain habits which another will rigidly abjure, and so on, plainly indicating that theological belief is not an influential factor in a man's life.

A man's theological belief is merely his intellectual opinion or view of the universe. God, The Bible, etc., and behind and underneath this head-belief there lies, deeply rooted in his innermost being, the hidden, silent, *secret belief of his heart,* and it is this belief which moulds and makes his whole life. It is this which makes those six men who, whilst holding the same theology, are yet so vastly at variance in their deeds— *they differ in the vital belief of the heart.*

What, then, is this heart-belief?

It is that which a man loves and clings to and fosters in his soul; for he thus loves and clings to and fosters in his heart, because he believes in them, and believing in them and loving them, he practises them; thus is his life the effect of his belief, but it has no relation to the particular creed which comprises his intellectual belief. One man clings to impure and immoral things because he believes in them; another does not cling to them because he has ceased to believe in them. A man cannot cling to anything unless he believes in it; belief always precedes action, therefore a man's deeds and life are the fruits of his belief.

The Priest and the Levite who passed by the injured and helpless man, held, no doubt, very strongly to the theological doctrines of their fathers—that was their intellectual belief—but in their hearts they did not believe in mercy, and so lived and acted accordingly. The good Samaritan may or may not have had any theological beliefs nor was it necessary that he should have; but in his heart he believed in mercy, and acted accordingly.

Strictly speaking, there are only two beliefs which vitally affect the life, and they are, *belief in good* and *belief in evil.*

He who believes in all those things that are good, will love them, and live in them; he who believes in those things that are impure and selfish, will love them, and cling to them. The tree is known by its fruits.

A man's beliefs about God, Jesus, and the Bible are one thing; his life, as bound up in his actions, is another; therefore a man's theological belief is of no consequence; but the thoughts which he harbours, his attitude of mind towards others, and his actions, these, and these only, determine and demonstrate whether the belief of a man's heart is fixed in the false or true.

9

THOUGHT AND ACTION

A s the fruit to the tree and the water to the spring, so is action to thought. It does not come into manifestation suddenly and without a cause. It is the result of a long and silent growth; the end of a hidden process which has long been gathering force. The fruit of the tree and the water gushing from the rock are both the effect of a combination of natural processes in air and earth which have long worked together in secret to produce the phenomenon; and the beautiful acts of enlightenment and the dark deeds of sin are both the ripened effects of trains of thought which have long been harboured in the mind.

The sudden falling, when greatly tempted, into some grievous sin by one who was believed, and who probably believed himself, to stand firm, is seen neither to be a sudden nor a causeless thing when the hidden process of thought which led up to it are revealed. The *falling* was merely the end, the outworking, the finished result of what commenced in the mind probably years before. The man had allowed a wrong thought to enter his mind; and a second and a third time he had welcomed it, and allowed it to nestle in his heart. Gradually he became accustomed to it, and cherished, and fondled, and tended it; and so it grew, until at last it attained such strength and force that it attracted to itself the opportunity which enabled it to burst forth and ripen into act. As falls the stately building whose foundations have been gradually undermined by the action of water, so at last falls the strong man who allows corrupt thoughts to creep into his mind and secretly undermine his character.

When it is seen that all sin and temptation are the natural outcome of the thoughts of the individual, the way to overcome sin and temptation becomes plain, and its achievement a near possibility, and, sooner or later, a certain reality; for if a man will admit, cherish, and brood upon thoughts that are pure and good, those thoughts, just as surely as the impure, will grow and gather force, and will at last attract to themselves the opportunities which will enable them to ripen into act.

"There is nothing hidden that shall not be revealed," and every thought that is harboured in the mind must, by virtue of the impelling force which is inherent in the universe, at last blossom into act good or bad according to its nature. The divine Teacher and the sensualist are both the product of their own thoughts, and have become what they are as the result of the seeds of thought which they have implanted, are allowed to fall, into the garden of the heart, and have afterwards watered, tended, and cultivated.

Let no man think he can overcome sin and temptation by wrestling with opportunity; he can only overcome them by purifying his thoughts; and if he will, day by day, in the silence of his soul, and in the performance of his duties, strenuously overcome all erroneous inclination, and put in its place thoughts that are true and that will endure the light, opportunity to do evil will give place to opportunity for accomplishing good, for a man can only attract that to him which is in harmony with his nature, and no temptation can gravitate to a man unless there is that in his heart which is capable of responding to it.

Guard well your thoughts, reader, for what you really are in your secret thoughts today, be it good or evil, you will, sooner or later, become in actual deed. He who unwearingly guards the portals of his mind against the intrusion of sinful thoughts, and occupies himself with loving thoughts, with pure, strong, and beautiful thoughts, will, when the season of their ripening comes, bring forth the fruits of gentle and holy deeds, and no temptation that can come against him shall find him unarmed or unprepared.

10

YOUR MENTAL ATTITUDE

As a being of thought, your dominant mental attitude will determine your condition in life. It will also be the gauge of your knowledge and the measures of your attainment. The so-called limitations of your nature are the boundary lines of your thoughts; they are self-erected fences, and can be drawn to a narrower circle, extended to a wider, or be allowed to remain.

You are the thinker of your thoughts and as such you are the maker of yourself and condition. Thought is causal and creative, and appears in your character and life in the form of results. There are no accidents in your life. Both its harmonies and antagonisms are the responsive echoes of your thoughts. A man thinks, and his life appears.

If your dominant mental attitude is peaceable and lovable, bliss and blessedness will follow you; if it be resistant and hateful, trouble and distress will cloud your pathway. Out of ill-will will come grief and disaster; out of good-will, healing and reparation.

You imagine your circumstances as being separate from yourself, but they are intimately related to your thought world. Nothing appears without an adequate cause. Everything that happens is just. Nothing is fated, everything is formed.

As you think, you travel; as you love, you attract. You are today where your thoughts have brought you; you will be tomorrow where your thoughts take you. You cannot escape the result of your thoughts, but you can endure and learn, can accept and be glad.

You will always come to the place where your love (your most abiding and intense thought) can receive its measure of gratification. If your love be base, you will come to a base place; if it be beautiful, you will come to a beautiful place. You can alter your thoughts, and so alter your condition. Strive to perceive the vastness and grandeur of your responsibility. You are powerful, not powerless. You are as powerful to obey as you are to disobey; as strong to be pure as to be impure; as ready for wisdom as for ignorance. You can learn what you will, can remain as ignorant as you choose. If you love knowledge you will obtain it; if you love wisdom you will secure it; if you love purity you will realise it. All things await your acceptance, and you choose by the thoughts which you entertain.

A man remains ignorant because he loves ignorance, and chooses ignorant thoughts; a man becomes wise because he loves wisdom and chooses wise thoughts. No man is hindered by another; he is only hindered by himself. No man suffers because of another; he suffers only because of himself. By the noble Gateway of Pure Thought you can enter the highest Heaven; by the ignoble doorway of impure thought you can descend into the lowest hell.

Your mental attitude towards others will faithfully react upon your - self, and will manifest itself in every relation of your life. Every impure and selfish thought that you send out comes back to you in your circumstances in some form of suffering; every pure and unselfish thought returns to you in some form of blessedness. Your circumstances are effects of which the cause is inward and invisible. As the father-mother of your thoughts you are the maker of your state and condition. When you know yourself, you will perceive, that every event in your life is weighed in the faultless balance of equity. When you understand the law within your mind you will cease to regard yourself as the impotent and blind tool of circum - stances, and will become the strong and seeing master.

11

SOWING AND REAPING

Go into the fields and country lanes in the spring-time, and you will see farmers and gardeners busy sowing seeds in the newly prepared soil. If you were to ask any one of those gardeners or farmers what kind of produce he expected from the seed he was sowing, he would doubt-less regard you as foolish, and would tell you that he does not "expect" at all, that it is a matter of common knowledge that his produce will be of the kind which he is sowing, and that he is sowing wheat, or barley, or turnips, as the case may be, in order to reproduce that particular kind.

Every fact and process in Nature contains a moral lesson for the wise man. There is no law in the world of Nature around us which is not to be found operating with the same mathematical certainty in the mind of man and in human life. All the parables of Jesus are illustrative of this truth, and are drawn from the simple facts of Nature. There is a process of seed-sowing in the mind and life a spiritual sowing which leads to a harvest according to the kind of seed sown. Thoughts, words, and acts are seeds sown, and, by the inviolable law of things, they produce after their kind.

The man who thinks hateful thoughts brings hatred upon himself. The man who thinks loving thoughts is loved. The man whose thoughts, words and acts are sincere, is surrounded by sincere friends; the insincere man is surrounded by insincere friends. The man who sows wrong thoughts and deeds, and prays that God will bless him, is in the position of a farmer who, having sown tares, asks God to bring forth for him a harvest of wheat.

That which ye sow, ye reap; see yonder fields
The sesamum was sesamum, the corn
Was corn; the silence and the darkness knew;
So is a man's fate born.
He cometh reaper of the things he sowed.

He who would be blest, let him scatter blessings. He who would be happy, let him consider the happiness of others.

Then there is another side to this seed sowing. The farmer must scatter all his seed upon the land, and then leave it to the elements. Were he to covetously hoard his seed, he would lose both it and his produce, for his seed would perish. It perishes when he sows it, but in perishing it brings forth a great abundance. So in life, we get by giving; we grow rich by scattering. The man who says he is in possession of knowledge which he cannot give out because the world is incapable of receiving it, either does not possess such knowledge, or, if he does, will soon be deprived of it—if he is not already so deprived. To hoard is to lose; to exclusively retain is to be dispossessed.

Even the man who would increase his material wealth must be willing to part with (invest) what little capital he has, and then wait for the increase. So long as he retains his hold on his precious money, he will not only remain poor, but will be growing poorer every day. He will, after all, lose the thing he loves, and will lose it without increase. But if he wisely lets it go; if, like the farmer, he scatters his seeds of gold, then he can faithfully wait for, and reasonably expect, the increase.

Men are asking God to give them peace and purity, and righteousness and blessedness, but are not obtaining these things; and why not? Because they are not practising them, not sowing them. I once heard a preacher pray very earnestly for forgiveness, and shortly afterwards, in the course of his sermon, he called upon his congregation to "show no mercy to the enemies of the church." Such self-delusion is pitiful, and men have yet to learn that the way to obtain peace and blessedness is to scatter peaceful and blessed thoughts, words, and deeds.

Men believe that they can sow the seeds of strife, impurity, and unbrotherliness, and then gather in a rich harvest of peace, purity and concord by merely asking for it. What more pathetic sight than to see an irritable and quarrelsome man praying for peace. Men reap that which they sow, and any man can reap all blessedness now and at once, if he will put aside selfishness, and sow broadcast the seeds of kindness, gentleness, and love.

If a man is troubled, perplexed, sorrowful, or unhappy, let him ask:

- "What mental seeds have I been sowing?"
- . "What seeds am I sowing?"
- "What have I done for others?"
- "What is my attitude towards others?"
- "What seeds of trouble and sorrow and unhappiness have I sown that I should thus reap these bitter weeds?"

Let him seek within and find, and having found, let him abandon all the seeds of self, and sow, henceforth, only the seeds of Truth.

Let him learn of the farmer the simple truths of wisdom.

12

The Reign of Law

The little party gods have had their day. The arbitrary gods, creatures of human caprice and ignorance, are falling into disrepute. Men have quarrelled over and defended them until they have grown weary of the strife, and now, everywhere, they are relinquishing and breaking up these helpless idols of their long worship.

The god of revenge, hatred and jealousy, who gloats over the downfall of his enemies; the partial god who gratifies all our narrow and selfish desires; the god who saves only the creatures of his particular special creed; the god of exclusiveness and favouritism; such were the gods (miscalled by us God) of our soul's infancy, gods base and foolish as ourselves, the fabrications of our selfish self. And we relinquished our petty gods with bitter tears and misgivings, and broke our idols with bleeding hands. But in so doing we did not lose sight of God; nay we drew nearer to the great, silent Heart of Love. Destroying the idols of self, we began to comprehend somewhat of the Power which cannot be destroyed, and entered into a wider knowledge of the God of Love, of Peace, of Joy; the God in whom revenge and partiality cannot exist; the God of Light, from whose presence the darkness of fear and doubt and selfishness cannot choose but flee.

We have reached one of those epochs in the world's progress which witnesses the passing of the false gods; the gods of human selfishness and human illusion. The new-old revelation of one universal impersonal Truth has again dawned upon the world, and its searching light has carried consternation to the perishable gods who take shelter under the shadow of self.

Men have lost faith in a god who can be cajoled, who rules arbitrarily and capriciously, subverting the whole order of things to gratify the wishes of his worshippers, and are turning, with a new light in their eyes and a new joy in their hearts, to the God of Law.

And to Him they turn, not for personal happiness and gratification, but for knowledge, for understanding, for wisdom, for liberation from the bondage of self. And thus turning, they do not seek in vain, nor are they sent away empty and discomfited. They find within themselves the reign of Law, that every thought, every impulse, every act and word brings about a result in exact accordance with its own nature; that thoughts of love bring about beautiful and blissful conditions, that hateful thoughts bring about distorted and painful conditions, that thoughts and acts good and evil are weighed in the faultless balance of the Supreme Law, and receive their equal measure of blessedness on the one hand, and misery on the other. And thus finding they enter a new Path, the Path of Obedience to the Law. Entering that Path they no longer accuse, no longer doubt, no longer fret and despond, for they know that God is right, the universal laws are right, the cosmos is right, and that they themselves are wrong, if wrong there is, and that their salvation depends upon themselves, upon their own efforts, upon their personal acceptance of that which is good and deliberate rejection of that which is evil. No longer merely hearers, they become doers of the Word, and they acquire knowledge, they receive understanding, they grow in wisdom, and they enter into the glorious life of liberation from the bondage of self.

"The Law of the Lord is perfect, enlightening the eyes." Imperfection lies in man's ignorance, in man's blind folly. Perfection, which is knowledge of the Perfect Law, is ready for all who earnestly seek it; it belongs to the order of things; it is yours and mine now if we will only put self-seeking on one side, and adopt the life of self-obliteration.

The knowledge of Truth, with its unspeakable joy, its calmness and quiet strength, is not for those who persist in clinging to their "rights," defending their "interests," and fighting for their "opinions"; whose works are imbued with the personal "I," and who build upon the shifting sands of selfishness and egotism. It is for those who renounce these causes of strife, these sources of pain and sorrow; and they are, indeed, Children of Truth, disciples of the Master, worshippers of the most High.

The Children of Truth are in the world today; they are thinking, acting, writing, speaking; yea, even prophets are amongst us, and their influence is pervading the whole earth. An undercurrent of holy joy is gathering force in the world, so that men and women are moved with new aspirations and hopes, and even those who neither see nor hear, feel within themselves strange yearnings after a better and fuller life.

The Law reigns, and it reigns in men's hearts and lives; and they have come to understand the reign of Law who have sought out the Tabernacle of the true God by the fair pathway of unselfishness.

God does not alter for man, for this would mean that the perfect must become imperfect; man must alter for God, and this implies that the imperfect must become perfect. The Law cannot be broken for man, otherwise confusion would ensue; man must obey the Law; this is in accordance with harmony, order, justice.

There is no more painful bondage than to be at the mercy of one's inclinations; no greater liberty than utmost obedience to the Law of Being. And the Law is that the heart shall be purified, the mind regenerated, and the whole being brought in subjection to Love till self is dead and Love is all in all, for the reign of Law is the reign of Love. And Love waits for all, rejecting none. Love may be claimed and entered into now, for it is the heritage of all.

Ah, beautiful Truth! To know that now man may accept his divine heritage, and enter the Kingdom of Heaven!

Oh, pitiful error! To know that man rejects it because of love of self!

Obedience to the Law means the destruction of sin and self, and the realisation of unclouded joy and undying peace.

Clinging to one's selfish inclinations means the drawing about one's soul clouds of pain and sorrow which darken the light of Truth; the shutting out of oneself from all real blessedness; for "whatsoever a man sows that shall he also reap."

Verily the Law reigneth, and reigneth for ever, and Justice and Love are its eternal ministers.

13

THE SUPREME JUSTICE

The material universe is maintained and preserved by the equilibrium of its forces.

The moral universe is sustained and protected by the perfect balance of its equivalents.

As in the physical world Nature abhors a vacuum, so in the spiritual world disharmony is annulled.

Underlying the disturbances and destructions of Nature, and behind the mutability of its forms, there abides the eternal and perfect mathematical symmetry; and at the heart of life, behind all its pain, uncertainty, and unrest, there abide the eternal harmony, the unbroken peace, and inviolable Justice.

Is there, then, no injustice in the universe? There is injustice, and there is not. It depends upon the kind of life and the state of con-sciousness from which a man looks out upon the world and judges. The man who lives in his passions sees injustice everywhere; the man who has overcome his passions, sees the operations of Justice in every department of human life. Injustice is the confused, feverish dream of passion, real enough to those who are dreaming it; Justice is the permanent reality in life, gloriously visible to those who have wakened out of the painful nightmare of self.

The Divine Order cannot be perceived until passion and self are transcended; the Faultless Justice cannot be apprehended until all sense of injury and wrong is consumed in the pure flames of all-embracing Love.

The man who thinks, "I have been slighted, I have been injured, I have been insulted, I have been treated unjustly," cannot know what Justice is; blinded by self, he cannot perceive the pure Principles of Truth, and brooding upon his wrongs, he lives in continual misery.

In the region of passion there is a ceaseless conflict of forces causing suffering to all who are involved in them. There is action and reaction, deed and consequence, cause and effect; and within and above all is the Divine Justice regulating the play of forces with the utmost mathematical accuracy, balancing cause and effect with the finest precision. But this Justice is not perceived—cannot be perceived—by those who are engaged in the conflict; before this can be done, the fierce warfare of passion must be left behind.

The world of passion is the abode of schisms, quarrellings, wars, law-suits, accusations, condemnations, impurities, weaknesses, follies, hatreds, revenges, and resentments. How can a man perceive Justice or understand Truth who is even partly involved in the fierce play of its blinding elements? As well expect a man caught in the flames of a burning building to sit down and reason out the cause of the fire.

In this realm of passion, men see injustice in the actions of others because, seeing only immediate appearances, they regard every act as standing by itself, undetached from cause and consequence. Having no knowledge of cause and effect in the moral sphere, men do not see the exacting and balancing process which is momentarily proceeding, nor do they ever regard their own actions as unjust, but only the actions of others. A boy beats a defenceless animal, then a man beats the defenceless boy for his cruelty, then a stronger man attacks the man for his cruelty to the boy. Each believes the other to be unjust and cruel, and himself to be just and humane; and doubtless most of all would the boy justify his conduct toward the animal as altogether necessary. Thus does ignorance keep alive hatred and strife; thus do men blindly inflict suffering upon themselves, living in passion and resentment, and not finding the true way in life. Hatred is met with hatred, passion with passion, strife with strife. The man who kills is himself killed; the thief who lives by depriving others is himself deprived; the beast that preys on others is hunted and killed; the accuser is accused, the condemner is condemned, the denouncer is persecuted.

> By this the slayer's knife doth stab himself,
> The unjust judge has lost his own defender,
> The false tongue dooms its lie, the creeping thief
> And spoiler rob to render.
> Such is the Law.

Passion also has its active and passive sides. Fool and fraud, oppressor and slave, aggressor and retaliator, the charlatan and the superstitious, complement each other, and come together by the operation of the Law of Justice. Men unconsciously cooperate in the mutual production of affliction; "the blind lead the blind, and both fall together into the ditch." Pain, grief, sorrow, and misery are the fruits of which passion is the flower.

Where the passion-bound soul sees only injustice, the good man, he who has conquered passion, sees cause and effect, sees the Supreme Justice. It is impossible for such a man to regard himself as treated unjustly, because he has ceased to see injustice. He knows that no one can injure or cheat him, having ceased to injure or cheat himself. However passionately or ignorantly men may act towards him, it cannot possibly cause him any pain, for he knows that whatever comes to him (it may be abuse and persecution) can only come as the effect of what he himself has formerly sent out. He therefore regards all things as good, rejoices in all things, loves his enemies and blesses them that curse him, regarding them as the blind but beneficent instruments by which he is enabled to pay his moral debts to the Great Law.

The good man, having put away all resentment, retaliation, self-seeking, and egotism, has arrived at a state of equilibrium, and has thereby become identified with the Eternal and Universal Equilibrium.

Having lifted himself above the blind forces of passion, he understands those forces, contemplates them with a calm penetrating insight, like the solitary dweller upon a mountain who looks down upon the conflict of the storms beneath his feet. For him, injustice has ceased, and he sees ignorance and suffering on the one hand and enlightenment and bliss on the other. He sees that not only do the fool and the slave need his sympathy, but that the fraud and the oppressor are equally in need of it, and so his compassion is extended towards all.

The Supreme Justice and the Supreme Love are one. Cause and effect cannot be avoided; consequences cannot be escaped.

While a man is given to hatred, resentment, anger and condemnation, he is subject to injustice as the dreamer to his dream, and cannot do otherwise than see injustice; but he who has overcome those fiery and binding elements, knows that unerring Justice presides over all, that in reality there is no such thing as injustice in the whole of the universe.

14

THE USE OF REASON

We have heard it said that reason is a blind guide, and that it draws men away from Truth rather than leads them to it. If this were true, it were better to remain, or to become, unreasonable, and to persuade others so to do. We have found, however, that the diligent cultivation of the divine faculty of reason brings about calmness and mental poise, and enables one to meet cheerfully the problems and difficulties of life.

It is true there is a higher light than reason; even that of the Spirit of Truth itself, but without the aid of reason, Truth cannot be apprehended. They who refuse to trim the lamp of reason will never, whilst they so refuse, perceive the light of Truth, for the light of reason is a reflection of that Light.

Reason is a purely abstract quality, and comes midway between the animal and divine consciousness in man, and leads, if rightly employed, from the darkness of one to the Light of the other. It is true that reason may be enlisted in the service of the lower, self-seeking nature, but this is only a result of its partial and imperfect exercise. A fuller development of reason leads away from the selfish nature, and ultimately allies the soul with the highest, the divine.

That spiritual Percival who, searching for the Holy Grail of the Perfect Life, is again and again

> *left alone,*
> *And wearying in a land of sand and thorns,*

is not so stranded because he has followed reason, but because he is still clinging to, and is reluctant to leave, some remnants of his lower nature. He who will use the light of reason as a torch to search for Truth will not be left at last in comfortless darkness.

"Come, now, and let us reason together, saith the Lord; though your sins be as scarlet, they shall be as white as snow."

Many men and women pass through untold sufferings, and at last die in their sins, because *they refuse to reason*; because they cling to those dark delusions which even a faint glimmer of the light of reason would dispel; and all must use their reason freely, fully, and faithfully, who would exchange the scarlet robe of sin and suffering for the white garment of blamelessness and peace.

It is because we have proved and know these truths that we exhort men to

> *tread the middle road, whose course*
> *Bright reason traces, and soft quiet*
> *smooths,*

for reason leads away from passion and selfishness into the quiet ways of sweet persuasion and gentle forgiveness, and he will never be led astray, nor will he follow blind guides, who faithfully adheres to the Apostolic injunction, "Prove all things, and hold fast that which is good." They, therefore, who despise the light of reason, despise the Light of Truth.

Large numbers of people are possessed of the strange delusion that reason is somehow intimately connected with the denial of the existence of God. This is probably due to the fact that those who try to prove that there is no God usually profess to take their stand upon reason, while those who try to prove the reverse generally profess to take their stand on faith. Such argumentative combatants, however, are frequently governed more by prejudice than either reason or faith, their object being not to find Truth, but to defend and confirm a pre-conceived opinion.

Reason is concerned, not with ephemeral opinions, but with the established truth of things, and he who is possessed of the faculty of reason in its purity and excellence can never be enslaved by prejudice, and will put from him all preconceived opinions as worthless. He will neither attempt to prove nor disprove, but after balancing extremes and bringing together all apparent contradictions, he will carefully and dispassionately weigh and consider them, and so arrive at Truth.

Reason is, in reality, associated with all that is pure and gentle, moderate and just. It is said of a violent man that he is "unreasonable," of a kind and considerate man that he is "reasonable," and of an insane man that he has "lost his reason." Thus it is seen that the word is used, even to a great extent unconsciously, though none the less truly, in a very comprehensive sense, and though reason is not actually love and thoughtfulness and gentleness and sanity, it leads to and is intimately connected with these divine qualities, and cannot, except for purposes of analysis, be dissociated from them.

Reason represents all that is high and noble in man. It distinguishes him from the brute which blindly follows its animal inclinations, and just in the degree that man disobeys the voice of reason and follows his inclinations does he become brutish. As Milton says:

> *Reason in man obscured, or not obeyed,*
> *Immediately inordinate desires*
> *And upstart passions catch the government*
> *From reason, and to servitude reduce*
> *Man till then free.*

The following definition of "reason" from Nuttall's Dictionary will give some idea of the comprehensiveness of the word:

> *The cause, ground, principle, or motive of anything said or done;*
> *efficient cause; final cause; the faculty of intelligence in man;*
> *especially the faculty by which we arrive at necessary truth.*

It will thus be seen that "reason" is a term, the breadth of which is almost sufficient to embrace even Truth itself, and Archbishop Trench tells us in his celebrated work *On the Study of Words** that the terms Reason and Word "are indeed so essentially one and the same that the Greek language has one word for them both," so that the Word of God is the Reason of God; and one of the renderings of Lao-tze's "Tao" is Reason, so that in the Chinese translation of our New Testament, St. John's Gospel runs, "In the beginning was the Tao."

To the undeveloped and uncharitable mind all words have narrow applications, but as a man enlarges his sympathies and broadens his intelligence, words become filled with rich meanings and assume comprehensive proportions. Let us therefore cease from foolish quarrellings about words, and, like reasonable beings, search for principles and practise those things which make for unity and peace.

---

*Allen's original text cites this work by Archbishop Trench, but the correct source is Trench's book *On the Authorized Version of the New Testament* (New York: Redfield, 1858).

15

SELF-DISCIPLINE

A man does not live until he begins to discipline himself; he merely exists. Like an animal he gratifies his desires and pursues his inclinations just where they may lead him. He is happy as a beast is happy, because he is not conscious of what he is depriving himself; he suffers as the beast suffers, because he does not know the way out of suffering. He does not intelligently reflect upon life, and lives in a series of sensations, longings, and confused memories which are unrelated to any central idea or principle. A man whose inner life is so ungoverned and chaotic must necessarily manifest this confusion in the visible conditions of his outer life in the world; and though for a time, running with the stream of his desires, he may draw to himself a more or less large share of the outer necessities and comforts of life, he never achieves any real success nor accomplishes any real good, and sooner or later worldly failure and disaster are inevitable, as the direct result of the inward failure to properly adjust and regulate those mental forces which make the outer life.

Before a man accomplish anything of an enduring nature in the world he must first of all acquire some measure of success in the management of his own mind. This is as mathematical a truism as that two and two are four, for, "out of the heart are the issues of life." If a man cannot govern the forces within himself, he cannot hold a firm hand upon the outer activities which form his visible life. On the other hand, as a man succeeds, in governing himself he rises to higher and higher levels of power and usefulness and success in the world.

The only difference between the life of the beast and that of the undisciplined man is that the man has a wider variety of desires, and experiences a greater intensity of suffering. It may be said of such a man that he is dead, being truly dead to self-control, chastity, fortitude, and all the nobler qualities which constitute life. In the consciousness of such a man the crucified Christ lies entombed, awaiting that resurrection which shall revivify the mortal sufferer, and wake him up to a knowl - edge of the realities of his existence.

With the practice of self-discipline a man begins to live, for he then commences to rise above the inward confusion and to adjust his conduct to a steadfast centre within himself. He ceases to follow where inclination leads him, reins in the steed of his desires, and lives in accordance with the dictates of reason and wisdom. Hitherto his life has been without purpose or meaning, but now he begins to consciously mould his own destiny; he is "clothed and in his right mind."

In the process of self-discipline there are three stages, namely:

1. Control
2. Purification
3. Relinquishment

A man begins to discipline himself by controlling those passions which have hitherto controlled him; he resists temptation and guards himself against all those tendencies to selfish gratifications which are so easy and natural, and which have formerly dominated him. He brings his appetite into subjection, and begins to eat as a reasonable and responsible being, practising moderation and thoughtfulness in the selection of his food, with the object of making his body a pure instrument through which he may live and act as becomes a man, and no longer degrading that body by pandering to gustatory pleasure. He puts a check upon his tongue, his temper, and, in fact, his every animal desire and tendency, and this he does by referring all his acts to a fixed centre within himself. It is a process of living from within outward, instead of, as formerly, from without inward. He conceives of an ideal, and, enshrining that ideal in the sacred recesses of his heart, he regulates his conduct in accordance with its exaction and demands.

There is a philosophical hypothesis that at the heart of every atom and every aggregation of atoms in the universe there is a *motionless centre* which is the sustaining source of all the universal activities. Be this as it may, there is certainly in the heart of every man and woman a selfless centre without which the outer man could not be, and the ignoring of which leads to suffering and confusion. This selfless centre which takes the form, in the mind, of an ideal of unselfishness and spotless purity, the attainment of which is desirable, is man's eternal refuge from the storms of passion and all the conflicting elements of his lower nature. It is the Rock of Ages, the Christ within, the divine and immortal in all men.

As a man practises self-control he approximates more and more to this inward reality, and is less and less swayed by passion and grief, pleasure and pain, and lives a steadfast and virtuous life, manifesting manly strength and fortitude. The restraining of the passions, however, is merely the initial stage in self-discipline, and is immediately followed by the process of Purification. By this a man so purifies himself as to take passion out of the heart and mind altogether; not merely restraining it when it rises within him, but preventing it from rising altogether. By merely restraining his passions a man can never arrive at peace, can never actualise his ideal; he must purify those passions.

It is in the purification of his lower nature that a man becomes strong and godlike, standing firmly upon the ideal centre within, and rendering all temptations powerless and ineffectual. This purification is effected by thoughtful care, earnest meditation, and holy aspiration; and as success is achieved confusion of mind and life pass away, and calmness of mind and spiritualized conduct ensure.

True strength and power and usefulness are born of self-purification, for the lower animal forces are not lost, but are transmuted into intellectual and spiritual energy. The pure life (pure in thought and deed) is a life of conservation of energy; the impure life (even should the impurity not extent beyond thought) is a life of dissipation of energy. The pure man is more capable, and therefore more fit to succeed in his plans and to accomplish his purposes than the impure. Where the impure man fails, the pure man will step in and be victorious, because he directs his energies with a calmer mind and a greater definiteness and strength of purpose.

With the growth in purity; all the elements which constitute a strong and virtuous manhood are developed in an increasing degree of power, and as a man brings his lower nature into subjection, and makes his passions do his bidding, just so much will he mould the outer circumstances of his life, and influence others for good.

The third stage of self-discipline, that of Relinquishment, is a process of letting the lower desires and all impure and unworthy thoughts drop out of the mind, and also refusing to give them any admittance, leaving them to perish. As a man grows purer, he perceives that all evil is powerless, unless it receives his encouragement, and so he ignores it, and lets it pass out of his life. It is by pursuing this aspect of self-discipline that a man enters into and realises the divine life, and manifests those qualities which are distinctly divine, such as wisdom, patience, non-resistance, compassion, and love. It is here, also, where a man becomes consciously immortal, rising above all the fluctuations and uncertainties of life, and living in and intelligent and unchangeable peace.

By self-discipline a man attains to every degree of virtue and holiness, and finally becomes a purified son of God, realising his oneness with the central heart of all things.

Without self-discipline a man drifts lower and lower, approximating more and more nearly to the beast, until at last he grovels, a lost creature, in the mire of his own befoulment. By self-discipline a man rises higher and higher, approximating more and more nearly to the divine, until at last he stands erect in his divine dignity, a saved soul, glorified by the radiance of his purity. Let a man discipline himself, and he will live; let a man cease to discipline himself, and he will perish.

As a tree grows in beauty, health, and fruitfulness by being carefully pruned and tended, so a man grows in grace and beauty of life by cutting away all the branches of evil from his mind, and as he tends and develops the good by constant and unfailing effort.

As a man by practice acquires proficiency in his craft, so the earnest man acquires proficiency in goodness and wisdom. Men shrink from self-discipline because in its early stages it is painful and repellent, and the yielding to desire is, at first, sweet and inviting; but the end of desire is darkness and unrest, whereas the fruits of discipline are immortality and peace.

16

RESOLUTION

Resolution is the directing and impelling force in individual progress. Without it no substantial work can be accomplished. Not until a man brings resolution to bear upon his life does he consciously and rapidly develop, for a life without resolution is a life without aims, and a life without aims is a drifting and unstable thing.

Resolution may of course be linked to downward tendencies, but it is more usually the companion of noble aims and lofty ideals, and I am dealing with it in this its highest use and application.

When a man makes a resolution, it means that he is dissatisfied with his condition, and is commencing to take himself in hand with a view to producing a better piece of workmanship out of the mental materials of which his character and life are composed, and in so far as he is true to his resolution he will succeed in accomplishing his purpose.

The vows of the saintly once are holy resolutions directed toward some victory over self, and the beautiful achievements of holy men and the glorious conquests of the Divine Teachers were rendered possible and actual by the pursuit of unswerving resolution.

To arrive at the fixed determination to walk a higher path than heretofore, although it reveals the great difficulties which have to be surmounted, it yet makes possible the treading of that path, and illuminates its dark places with the golden halo of success.

The true resolution is the crisis of long thought, protracted struggle, or fervent but unsatisfied aspiration. It is no light thing, no whimsical impulse or vague desire, but a solemn and irrevocable determination not to rest nor cease from effort until the high purpose which is held in view is fully accomplished.

Half-hearted and premature resolution is no resolution at all, and is shattered at the first difficulty.

A man should be slow to form a resolution. He should searchingly examine his position and take into consideration every circumstance and difficulty connected with his decision, and should be fully prepared to meet them. He should be sure that he completely understands the nature of his resolution, that his mind is finally made up, and that he is without fear and doubt in the matter. With the mind thus prepared, the resolution that is formed will not be departed from, and by the aid of it a man will, in due time, accomplish his strong purpose.

Hasty resolutions are futile.

The mind must be fortified to endure.

Immediately the resolution to walk a higher path is made, temptation and trial begin. Men have found that no sooner have they decided to lead a truer and nobler life than they have been overwhelmed with such a torrent of new temptations and difficulties as make their position almost unendurable, and many men, because of this, relinquish their resolution.

But these temptations and trials are a necessary part of the work of regeneration upon which the man has decided and must be hailed as friends and met with courage if the resolution is to do its work. For what is the real nature of a resolution? Is it not the sudden checking of a particular stream of conduct, and the endeavour to open up an entirely new channel? Think of an engineer who decides to turn the course of a powerfully running stream or river in another direction. He must first cut his new channel, and must take every precaution to avoid failure in the carrying out of his undertaking. But when he comes to the all-important task of directing the stream into its new channel, then the flowing force, which for ages has steadily pursued its accustomed course, becomes refractory, and all the patience and care and skill of the engineer will be required for the successful completion of the work. It is even so with the man who determines to turn his course of conduct in another and higher direction. Having prepared his mind, which is the cutting of a new channel, he then proceeds to the work of redirecting his mental forces—which have hitherto flowed on uninterruptedly—into the new course. Immediately this is attempted, the arrested energy begins to assert itself in the form of powerful temptations and trials hitherto unknown and unencountered. And this is exactly as it should be; it is the law; and the same law that is in the water is in the mind. No man can improve upon the established law of things, but he can learn to understand the law instead of complaining, and wishing things were different. The man who understands all that is involved in the regeneration of his mind will "glory in tribulations," knowing that only by passing through them can he gain strength, obtain purity of heart, and arrive at peace. And as the engineer at last (perhaps after many mistakes and failures) succeeds in getting the stream to flow on peacefully in the broader and better channel, and the turbulence of the water is spent, and all dams can be removed, so the man of resolution at last succeeds in directing his thoughts and acts into the better and nobler way to which he aspires, and temptations and trials give place to steadfast strength and settled peace.

He whose life is not in harmony with his conscience and who is anxious to remedy his mind and conduct in a particular direction, let him first mature his purpose by earnest thought and self-examination, and having arrived at a final conclusion, let him frame his resolution, and having done so let him not swerve from it, let him remain true to his decision under all circumstances, and he cannot fail to achieve his good purpose; for the Great Law ever shields and protects him who, no matter how deep his sins, or how great and many his failures and mistakes, has, deep in his heart, resolved upon the finding of a better way, and every obstacle must at last give way before a matured and unshaken resolution.

17

THE GLORIOUS CONQUEST

Truth can only be apprehended by the conquest of self.

Blessedness can only be arrived at by overcoming the lower nature.

The way of Truth is barred by a man's self.

The only enemies that can actually hinder him are his own passions and delusions. Until a man realises this, and commences to cleanse his heart, he has not found the Path which leads to knowledge and peace.

Until passion is transcended, Truth remains unknown. This is the Divine Law. A man cannot keep his passions and have Truth as well.

Error is not slain until selfishness is dead.

The overcoming of self is no mystical theory, but a very real and practical thing.

It is a process which must be pursued daily and hourly, with unswerv - ing faith and undaunted resolution if any measure of success is to be achieved.

The process is one of orderly growth, having its sequential stages, like the growth of a tree; and as fruit can only be produced by carefully and patiently training the tree even so the pure and satisfying fruits of holiness can only be obtained by faithfully and patiently training the mind in the growth of right thought and conduct.

There are five steps in the overcoming of passion (which includes all bad habits and particular forms of wrong-doing) which I will call:

1. Repression
2. Endurance
3. Elimination
4. Understanding
5. Victory

When men fail to overcome their sins, it is because they try to begin at the wrong end. They want to have the stage of Victory without passing through the previous four stages. They are in the position of a gardener who wants to produce good fruit without training and attending to his trees.

Repression consists in checking and controlling the wrong act (such as an outburst of temper, a hasty or unkind word, a selfish indulgence etc.), and not allowing it to take actual form. This is equivalent to the gardener nipping off the useless buds and branches from his tree. It is a necessary process, but a painful one. The tree bleeds while undergoing the process, and the gardener knows that it must not be taxed too severely. The heart also bleeds when it refuses to return passion for passion, when it ceases to defend and justify itself. It is the process of "mortifying the members" of which St. Paul speaks.

But this repression is only the beginning of self-conquest. When it is made an end in itself, and there is no object of finally purifying the heart, that is a stage of hypocrisy; a hiding of one's true nature, and striving to appear better in the eyes of others than one really is. In that case it is an evil, but when adopted as the first stage toward complete purification, it is good. Its practice leads to the second stage of *Endurance*, or forbearance, in which one silently endures the pain which arises in the mind when it is brought in contact with certain actions and attitudes of other minds toward one. As success is attained in this stage, the striver comes to see that all his pain actually arises in his own weaknesses, and not in the wrong attitudes of others toward him, these

latter being merely the means by which his sins are brought to the surface and revealed to him. He thus gradually exonerates all others from
blame in his falls and lapses of conduct, and accuses only himself, and so
learns to love those who thus unconsciously reveal to him his sins and
shortcomings.

Having passed through these two stages of self-crucifixion, the disciple enters the third, that of *Elimination*, in which the wrong thought
which lay behind the wrong act is cast from the mind immediately as it
appears. At this stage, conscious strength and holy joy begin to take
the place of pain, and the mind having become comparatively calm, the
striver is enabled to gain a deeper insight into the complexities of his
mind, and thus to understand the inception, growth, and outworking of
sin. This is the stage of *Understanding*.

Perfection in understanding leads to the final conquest of self, a
conquest so complete that the sin can no more rise in the mind even as
a thought or impression; for when the knowledge of sin is complete;
when it is known in its totality, from its inception as a seed in the mind
to its ripened outgrowth as act and consequence, then it can no more
be allowed a place in life, but it is abandoned for ever. Then the mind is
at peace. The wrong acts of others no longer arouse wrong and pain in
the mind of the disciple. He is glad and calm and wise. He is filled with
Love, and blessedness abides with him. And this is *Victory*!

18

CONTENTMENT IN ACTIVITY

The confounding of a positive spiritual virtue or principle with a negative animal vice is common amongst writers even of what is called the "Advance Thought School," and much valuable energy is frequently expended in criticising and condemning, where a little calm reasoning would have revealed a greater light, and led to the exercise of a broader charity.

The other day I came across a vigorous attack upon the teaching of "Love," wherein the writer condemned such teaching as weakly, foolish, and hypocritical. Needless to say, that which he was condemning as "Love," was merely weak sentimentality and hypocrisy.

Another writer in condemning "meekness" does not know that what he calls meekness is only cowardice, while another who attacks "chastity" as "a snare," is really confusing painful and hypocritical restraint with the virtue of chastity. And just lately I received a long letter from a correspondent who took great pains to show me that "contentment" is a vice, and is the source of innumerable evils.

That which my correspondent called "contentment" is, of course *animal indifference*. The spirit of indifference is incompatible with progress, whereas the spirit of contentment may, and does, attend the highest form of activity, the truest advancement and development.

Indolence is the twin sister of indifference, but cheerful and ready action is the friend of contentment.

Contentment is a virtue which becomes lofty and spiritual in its later developments, as the mind is trained to perceive and the heart to receive the guidance, in all things, of a merciful law.

To be contented does not mean to forego effort; it means to *free effort from anxiety*; it does not mean to be satisfied with sin and ignorance and folly, but to rest happily in duty done, work accomplished.

A man may be said to be content to lead a grovelling life, to remain in sin and in debt, but such a man's true state is one of indifference to his duty, his obligations, and the just claims of his fellow-men. He cannot truly be said to possess the virtue of contentment; he does not experience the pure and abiding joy which is the accompaniment of active contentment; so far as his true nature is concerned he is a sleeping soul, and sooner or later will be awakened by intense suffering, having passed through which he will find that true contentment which is the outcome of honest effort and true living.

There are three things with which a man should be content:

1. With whatever happens.
2. With his friendships and possessions.
3. With his pure thoughts.

Contented with whatever happens, he will escape grief; with his friends and possessions, he will avoid anxiety and wretchedness; and with his pure thoughts, he will never go back to suffer and grovel in impurities.

There are three things with which a man should not be content:

1. With his opinions.
2. With his character.
3. With his spiritual condition.

Not content with his opinions, he will continually increase in intelligence; not content with his character, he will ceaselessly grow in strength and virtue; and not content with his spiritual condition, he will, every day, enter into a larger wisdom and fuller blessedness. In a word, a man should be contented, but not indifferent to his development as a responsible and spiritual being.

The truly contented man works energetically and faithfully, and accepts all results with an untroubled spirit, trusting, at first, that all is well, but afterwards, with the growth of enlightenment, knowing that results exactly correspond with efforts. Whatsoever material possessions come to him, come not by greed and anxiety and strife, but by right thought, wise action, and pure exertion.

19

THE TEMPLE OF BROTHERHOOD

Universal Brotherhood is the supreme Ideal of Humanity, and towards that Ideal the world is slowly but surely moving.

Today, as never before, numbers of earnest men and women are striving to make this Ideal tangible and real; Fraternities are springing up on every hand, and Press and Pulpit, the world over, are preaching the Brotherhood of Man.

The unselfish elements in all such efforts cannot fail to have their effect upon the race, and are with certainty urging it towards the goal of its noblest aspirations; but the ideal state has not yet manifested through any outward organisation, and societies formed for the purpose of propagating Brotherhood are continually being shattered to pieces by internal dissension.

The Brotherhood for which Humanity sighs is withheld from actuality by Humanity itself; nay, more, it is frustrated even by men who work zealously for it is a desirable possibility; and this because the purely *spiritual* nature of Brotherhood is not perceived, and the principles involved, as well as the individual course of conduct necessary to perfect unity, are not comprehended.

Brotherhood as a human organisation cannot exist so long as any degree of self-seeking reigns in the hearts of men and women who band themselves together for any purpose, as such self-seeking must eventually rend the Seamless Coat of loving unity. But although organised Brotherhood has so far largely failed, any man may realise Brotherhood in its perfection, and know it in all its beauty and completion, if he will make himself of a wise, pure, and loving spirit, removing from his mind every element of strife, and learning to practise those divine qualities without which Brotherhood is but a mere theory, opinion, or illusive dream.

For Brotherhood is at first spiritual, and its outer manifestation in the world must follow as a natural sequence.

As a spiritual reality it must be discovered by each man for himself, and in the only place where spiritual realities can be found—*within himself*—and it rests with each whether he shall choose or refuse it.

There are four chief tendencies in the human mind which are destructive of Brotherhood, and which bar the way to its comprehension, namely:

1. Pride
2. Self-love
3. Hatred
4. Condemnation

Where these are there can be no Brotherhood; in whatsoever heart these hold sway, discord rules, and Brotherhood is not realised, for these tendencies are, in their very nature, dark and selfish and always make for disruption and destruction. From these four things proceeds that serpent brood of false actions and conditions which poison the heart of man, and fill the world with suffering and sorrow.

Out of the spirit of *pride* proceed envy, resentment, and opinionativeness. Pride envies the position, influence, or goodness of others; it thinks, "I am more deserving than this man or this woman"; it also continually finds occasion for resenting the actions of others, and says, "I have been snubbed," "I have been insulted," and thinking altogether of his own excellence, it sees no excellence in others.

From the spirit of *self-love* proceed egotism, lust for power, and disparagement and contempt. Self-love worships the personality in which it moves; it is lost in the adoration and glorification of that "I," that "self" which has no real existence, but is a dark dream and a delusion. It desires pre-eminence over others, and thinks, "I am great," "I am more important than others"; it also disparages others, and bestows upon them contempt, seeing no beauty in them, being lost in the contemplation of its own beauty.

From the spirit of *hatred* proceed slander, cruelty, reviling, and anger. It strives to overcome evil by adding evil to it. It says, "This man has spoken of me ill, I will speak still more ill of him and thus teach him a lesson." It mistakes cruelty for kindness, and causes its possessor to revile a reproving friend. It feeds the flames of anger with bitter and rebellious thoughts.

From the spirit of *condemnation* proceed accusation, false pity, and false judgement. It feeds itself on the contemplation of evil, and cannot see the good. It has eyes for evil only, and finds it in almost every thing and every person. It sets up an arbitrary standard of right and wrong by which to judge others, and it thinks, "This man does not do as I would have him do, he is therefore evil, and I will denounce him." So blind is the spirit of condemnation that whilst rendering its possessor incapable of judging himself, it causes him to set himself up as the judge of all the earth.

From the four tendencies enumerated, no element of brotherliness can proceed. They are deadly mental poisons, and he who allows them to rankle in his mind, cannot apprehend the peaceful principles on which Brotherhood rests.

Then there are chiefly four divine qualities which are productive of Brotherhood; which are, as it were, the foundation stones on which it rests, namely:

1. Humility
2. Self-surrender
3. Love
4. Compassion

Wheresoever these are, there Brotherhood is active. In whatsoever heart these qualities are dominant, there Brotherhood is an established reality, for they are, in their very nature, unselfish and are filled with the revealing Light of Truth. There is no darkness in them, and where they are, so powerful is their light, that the dark tendencies cannot remain, but are dissolved and dissipated. Out of these four qualities proceed all those angelic actions and conditions which make for unity and bring gladness to the heart of man and to the world.

From the spirit of Humility proceed meekness and peacefulness; from self-surrender come patience, wisdom, and true judgement; from Love spring kindness, joy, and harmony; and from Compassion proceed gentleness and forgiveness.

He who has brought himself into harmony with these four qualities is divinely enlightened; he sees whence the actions of men proceed and whither they tend, and therefore can no longer live in the exercise of the dark tendencies. He has realised Brotherhood in its completion as freedom from malice; from envy, from bitterness, from contention, from condemnation. All men are his brothers, those who live in the dark tendencies, as well as those who live in the enlightened qualities, for he knows that when they have perceived the glory and beauty of the Light of Truth, the dark tendencies will be dispelled from their minds. He has but one attitude of mind towards all, that of good-will.

Of the four dark tendencies are born ill-will and strife; of the four divine qualities are born good-will and peace.

Living in the four tendencies a man is a strife-producer. Living in the four qualities a man is a peace-maker.

Involved in the darkness of the selfish tendencies, men believe that they can fight for peace, kill to make alive, slay injury by injuring, restore love by hatred, unity by contention, kindness by cruelty, and establish brotherhood by erecting their own opinions (which they themselves will, in the course of time, abandon as worthless) as objects of universal adoration.

The wished-for Temple of Brotherhood will be erected in the world when its four foundation stones of Humility, Self-surrender,

Love, and Compassion are firmly laid in the hearts of men, for Brother-hood consists, first of all, in the abandonment of self by the individual, and its after-effects is unity between man and man.

Theories and schemes for propagating Brotherhood are many, but Brotherhood itself is one and unchangeable and consists in the complete cessation from egotism and strife, and in practising good-will and peace; for Brotherhood is a practice and not a theory. Self-surrender and Good-will are its guardian angels, and peace is its habitation.

Where two are determined to maintain an opposing opinion, the clinging to self and ill-will are there, and Brotherhood is absent. Where two are prepared to sympathise with each other, to see no evil in each other, to serve and not to attack each other; the Love of Truth and Good-will are there, and Brotherhood is present.

All strifes, divisions, and wars inhere in the proud, unyielding self; all peace, unity, and concord inhere in the Principles which the yielding up of self reveals. Brotherhood is only practised and known by him whose heart is at peace with all the world.

20

PLEASANT PASTURES OF PEACE

He who aspires to the bettering of himself and humanity should ceaselessly strive to arrive at the exercise of that blessed attitude of mind by which he is enabled to put himself, mentally and sympathetically in the place of others, and so, instead of harshly and falsely judging them, and thereby making himself unhappy without adding to the happiness of those others, he will enter into their experience, will understand their particular frame of mind, and will feel for them and sympathise with them.

One of the great obstacles to the attainment of such an attitude of mind is prejudice, and until this is removed it is impossible to act toward others as we would wish others to act toward us.

Prejudice is destructive of kindness, sympathy, love and true judgement, and the strength of a man's prejudice will be the measure of his harshness and unkindness toward others, for prejudice and cruelty are inseparable.

There is no rationality in prejudice, and, immediately it is aroused in a man he ceases to act as a reasonable being, and gives way to rashness, anger, and injurious excitement. He does not consider his words nor regard the feelings and liberties of those against whom his prejudices are directed. He has, for the time being, forfeited his manhood, and has descended to the level of an irrational creature.

While a man is determined to cling to his preconceived opinions, mistaking them for Truth, and refuses to consider dispassionately the position of others, he cannot escape hatred nor arrive at blessedness.

The man who strives after gentleness, who aspires to act unselfishly toward others, will put away all his passionate prejudice and petty opinions, and will gradually acquire the power of thinking and feeling for others, of understanding their particular state of ignorance or knowledge, and thereby entering fully into their hearts and lives, sympathizing with them and seeing them as they are.

Such a man will not oppose himself to the prejudices of others by introducing his own, but will seek to allay prejudice by introducing sympathy and love, striving to bring out all that is good in men, encouraging the good by appealing to it, and discouraging the evil by ignoring it. He will realise the good in the unselfish efforts of others, though their outward methods may be very different from his own, and will so rid his heart of hatred, and will fit it with love and blessedness.

When a man is prone to harshly judge and condemn others, he should inquire how far he falls short himself; he should also reconsider those periods of suffering when he himself was misjudged and misunderstood, and, gathering wisdom and love from his own bitter experience, should studiously and self-sacrificingly refrain from piercing with anguish hearts that are as yet too weak to ignore, too immature and uninstructed to understand.

Sympathy is not required towards those who are purer and more enlightened than one's self, as the purer one lives above the necessity for it. In such a case reverence should be exercised, with a striving to lift one's self up to the purer level, and so enter into possession of the larger life. Nor can a man fully understand one who is wiser than himself, and before condemning, he should earnestly ask himself whether he is, after all, better than the man whom he has singled out as the object of his bitterness. If he is, let him bestow sympathy. If he is not, let him exercise reverence.

For thousands of years the sages have taught, both by precept and example, that evil is only overcome by good, yet still that lesson for the majority, remains unlearned. It is a lesson profound in its simplicity, and difficult to learn because men are blinded by the illusions of self. Men are still engaged in resenting, condemning, and fighting the evil in their own fellow-men, thereby increasing the delusion in their own hearts, and adding to the world's sum of misery and suffering. When they find out that their own resentment must be eradicated, and love put in its place, evil will perish for lack of sustenance.

> *With burning brain and heart of hate,*
> *I sought my wronger, early, late,*
> *And all the wretched night and day*
> *My dream and thought was slay, and slay.*
> *My better self rose uppermost,*
> *The beast within my bosom lost*
> *Itself in love; peace from afar*
> *Shone o'er me radiant like a star.*
> *I Slew my wronger with a deed,*
> *A deed of love; I made him bleed*
> *With kindness, and I filled for years*
> *His soul with tenderness and tears.*

Dislike, resentment, and condemnation are all forms of hatred, and evil cannot cease until these are taken out of the heart.

But the obliterating of injuries from the mind is merely one of the beginnings in wisdom. There is a still higher and better way. And that way is so to purify the heart and enlighten the mind that, far from having to forget injuries, there will be none to remember. For it is only pride and self that can be injured and wounded by the actions and attitudes of others; and he who takes pride and self out of his heart can never think the thought, "I have been injured by another" or "I have been wronged by another."

From a purified heart proceeds the right comprehension of things; and from the right comprehension of things proceeds the life that is peaceful, freed from bitterness and suffering, calm and wise. He who thinks, "This man has injured me," has not perceived the Truth in life; falls short of that enlightenment which disperses the erroneous idea of evil as a thing to be hatefully resented. He who is troubled and disturbed about the sins of others is far from Truth; he who is troubled and disturbed about his own sins is very near to the Gate of Wisdom. He in whose heart the flames of resentment burn, cannot know Peace nor understand Truth; he who will banish resentment from his heart, will know and understand.

He who has taken evil out of his own heart cannot resent or resist it in others, for he is enlightened as to its origin and nature, and knows it as a manifestation of the mistakes of ignorance. With the increase of enlightenment, sin becomes impossible. He who sins, does not understand; he who understands does not sin.

The pure man maintains his tenderness of his heart toward those who ignorantly imagine they can do him harm. The wrong attitude of others toward him does not trouble him; his heart is at rest in Compassion and Love.

Blessed is he who has no wrongs to remember, no injuries to forget; in whose pure heart no hateful thought about another can take root and flourish. Let those who aim at the right life, who believe that they love Truth, cease to passionately oppose themselves to others, and let them strive to calmly and wisely understand them, and in thus acting toward others they will be conquering themselves; and while sympathizing with others, their own souls will be fed with the heavenly dews of kindness, and their hearts be strengthened and refreshed in the Pleasant Pastures of Peace.